THE TRUE STORY OF
J. EDGAR
HOOVER
AND THE FBI

★★★★★★★★★★★

FBI

Also by
BARRY DENENBERG

Nelson Mandela:
"No Easy Walk to Freedom"

John Fitzgerald Kennedy:
America's 35th President

Stealing Home:
The Story of Jackie Robinson

THE TRUE STORY OF
J. EDGAR HOOVER AND THE FBI

★★★★★★★★★★★

BY BARRY DENENBERG

SCHOLASTIC
HARDCOVER

SCHOLASTIC INC.
New York

to Bob and Mary Mills,
who showed me the way

LIBRARY OF CONGRESS CATALOGING-IN-PUBLICATION DATA
Denenberg, Barry.   The True Story of J. Edgar Hoover and the FBI / Barry Denenberg.
p.   cm.   Includes bibliographical references and index.   Summary: A biography of the former chief of the Federal Bureau of Investigation, focusing on the FBI's impact on the major law enforcement issues of the 1920s through the early 1970s.

ISBN 0-590-43168-4

1. United States. Federal Bureau of Investigation—History—Juvenile literature.   2. Hoover, J. Edgar (John Edgar), 1895–1972—Juvenile literature.   3. Police—United States— Biography—Juvenile literature.   [1. Hoover, J. Edgar (John Edgar), 1895–1972.   2. Police. 3. United States. Federal Bureau of Investigation—History.]   I. Title.
HV8144.F43D46   1991   91-8021   CIP
353.0074'09—dc20   AC

12 11 10 9 8 7 6 5 4 3 2 1   3 4 5 6 7 8/9
Printed in the U.S.A.   23
First Scholastic printing, April 1993

CONTENTS

INTRODUCTION
★

THE WIZARD OF WASHINGTON

". . . wielded more power, longer, than any man
in American history."

Journalist Tom Wicker

In September, 1965, *The FBI* premiered on ABC-TV. Every Sunday night at eight o'clock, Inspector Louis Erskine and his fellow FBI agents solved difficult cases with ease and efficiency. The FBI created by Hollywood always got its man. The message was clear: crime did not pay.

The FBI agents portrayed on TV were, in many ways, like their real-life counterparts: white, middle-class, and male; clean-shaven family men with close-cropped haircuts, white shirts, ties, and neatly pressed suits. They didn't smoke or drink and were, above all, loyal to the Federal Bureau of Investigation.

Viewers (at its peak, forty million people watched the show each week) saw agents who were patient and polite; trustworthy, honest men who operated within the letter and spirit of the law. They worked smoothly with local authorities to put those who violated federal laws where they belonged: behind bars. Inspector Erskine and his men were dedicated to protecting American citizens from forces considered too powerful for

1

the state and local police. For a whole generation of Americans, *The FBI* represented what they thought was an accurate account of the real FBI in action.

This was no accident. Longtime FBI Director J. Edgar Hoover had made sure that viewers saw the FBI he wanted them to see. Hoover monitored the television series as closely as he monitored the real FBI. No detail escaped his attention and nothing was left to chance.

Before allowing the series to be produced, Hoover had insisted that he be given complete approval of the show's scripts. These scripts, which were based on actual FBI cases, were first submitted to the FBI's Los Angeles field office and then sent to Washington for final approval.

During the filming, FBI agents were on hand to ensure that nothing took place of which Hoover might disapprove. If an actor didn't question a witness or suspect in exactly the way an FBI agent should, changes were made. If he didn't hold his weapon properly, he was shown how to. In one case, it was suggested that an "agent" was driving his car too fast, and the speed was reduced.

All four of the principal actors in the series were given routine background checks to make sure there was nothing in their backgrounds that might embarrass the bureau. The actor playing Inspector Erskine had been handpicked by Hoover. Everyone on the set, carpenters and electricians included, had to be cleared by the FBI.

In 1971, with *The FBI* in its sixth season, a burglary occurred that would eventually prove that the real FBI operated differently from the TV FBI.

On March 8, 1971, in the middle of the night, the FBI field office in Media, Pennsylvania, was broken into. The burglars knocked down the door of a second-floor office and then forced open a filing cabinet. Security was lax and no alarm sounded. In the morning, when FBI employees arrived, they found the Domestic Security files missing.

Excerpts from these documents began appearing in major newspapers, such as *The New York Times* and *The Washington Post*. It was the first time that actual FBI files had been read by the American public.

The curtain of secrecy surrounding J. Edgar Hoover and the FBI had been torn aside. Hoover, like the Wizard of Oz, was suddenly revealed pulling levers, twisting dials, and pushing buttons as he manipulated the vast machinery of the Federal Bureau of Investigation. However, unlike the Wizard of Oz, it wasn't a *lack* of secret powers the Wizard of Washington was hiding. On the contrary, his power had grown too great. The FBI, it appeared, had been operating outside of the law in a variety of areas.

Under Hoover's ironfisted rule, the Federal Bureau of Investigation illegally surveilled and attacked people whose beliefs the director disagreed with, but who were not violating any laws. The Media, Pennsylvania, documents showed, for the first time, the extremes to which Hoover had gone. They showed the degree to which he had abused the power that he had been able to amass.

For years, the FBI had been immune to criticism. But in the coming years, Hoover would be revealed as a man who had become a law unto himself. He alone decided who were the bad guys and who were the good guys.

Today, the J. Edgar Hoover FBI Building is one of the most popular tourist stops in Washington, DC, the nation's capital. Hoover's portrait hangs alongside those FBI directors who have come before him and those who have served since. Hoover, however, was unique.

He alone built the FBI's worldwide reputation and was himself considered an authority on crime detection. Widely regarded as the nation's

The FBI Building in Washington, DC

top law enforcement officer, Hoover had, however, never personally investigated a case. He ran the FBI for nearly half a century, during the administrations of *eight* presidents. When he first took over the bureau, it took 27 hours to fly from New York to San Francisco. When he died, forty-eight years later and still director of the FBI, the Apollo 16 astronauts had spent 71 hours on the moon.

The story of J. Edgar Hoover and the FBI spans American history from World War I to the Vietnam War. It begins almost a hundred years ago — at the turn of the century — when there was no Federal Bureau of Investigation.

PART ONE

★

THE YEARS OF GROWTH

"No one need erect a monument to you. You have built your own monument in the form of the FBI — for the FBI is J. Edgar Hoover and I think we can rest assured that it will always be."

Senator Joseph McCarthy

CHAPTER ONE

★

THE BUREAU BEFORE HOOVER

"In my reading of history I recall no instance where a government has perished because of the absence of a secret-service force, but many there are that perished as a result of a spy system. If Anglo-Saxon civilization stands for anything, it is for a government where the humblest citizen is safeguarded against the secret activities of the executive of the government."

Congressman J. Swagar Sherley

In 1870, the Justice Department was created to investigate and prosecute crimes against the United States. By 1908, the year the Bureau of Investigation was established, the department's responsibilities had increased and become more complex. The Justice Department, headed by the attorney general, was responsible for investigating:

- Antitrust violations: when companies conspired together to drive their competitors out of business
- Fraudulent land sales: when land thieves out west illegally sold public land for private profit
- Peonage crimes: in which people were made slaves in order to pay off their debts
- Crimes on Indian reservations, which were federal property
- The shipment of stolen goods from one state to another
- Violations of the national banking laws

Yet the Justice Department had to borrow detectives from other bureaus, such as Customs, the Department of the Interior, and, most often, the Treasury Department (the Treasury Department had a police force to protect its money-minting operations).

When Theodore Roosevelt was president, his Attorney General Charles Bonaparte (a grandnephew of the French Emperor Napoleon I), asked Congress for funds to hire a detective force for the Justice Department. Bonaparte stated that he wanted to set professional standards and employ men in permanent positions. He felt that the Justice Department was unable to do its job properly. He complained that "a Department of Justice with no force of permanent police . . . is . . . not fully equipped for its work."

Critics feared that President Roosevelt, or later presidents, would use the bureau for personal political reasons. This new investigative force might be used to keep a president in power, force others out of power, or suppress opposition. Bonaparte told the congressmen he understood that it would be tempting to use the bureau for political purposes, but he was sure it would never be done. He listed safeguards to prevent such abuses:

- Only professional investigators would be hired.
- The attorney general would assume direct supervisory responsibility.
- The bureau would not investigate political beliefs or personal matters.
- Investigations would be confined to violations of antitrust and interstate commerce laws.

Many members of Congress were opposed to the formation of a permanent investigative force: ". . . we will have in time a Federal secret police," said a Minnesota congressman. "It is considered absolutely contradictory to the democratic principles of government," a Chicago paper editorialized.

The struggle over the creation of the Bureau of Investigation involved two basic issues of American government. One, Congress saw Bonaparte's proposal as an unwanted expansion of the power of the president. A balance of power among the legislative, executive, and judicial branches of government was one of the principles upon which the country was founded. The second issue raised an even more fundamental question: Was the establishment of what might become a secret police force something that the founding fathers had tried to prevent? The Fourth Amendment to the Constitution states: "The right of the people to be secure in their persons, houses, papers, and effects, against unreasonable searches and seizures, shall not be violated."

Congress turned down Bonaparte's request but, with the president's support, he went forward anyway, using funds already available to him. In the summer of 1908, the Bureau of Investigation, later called the Federal Bureau of Investigation, was established.

The bureau's first fifteen years were shaky ones. Despite Bonaparte's assurances, there were no standards for hiring and little direction. Many of the bureau's early activities proved to be embarrassing. Agents were not even permitted to carry guns.

BLACK TOM ISLAND

World War I had been raging in Europe for about three years before the United States entered on April 6, 1917. Although the United States was, during those three years, officially neutral, it had become "the arsenal of democracy." American industry had already become the chief armament supplier for Britain and France in their fight against Germany.

Black Tom Island, in New York Harbor across from the Statue of

Liberty, served as a mammoth munitions depot. At 2:00 A.M. on Sunday, July 30, 1916, the Manhattan skyline was lit up orange-red as a monstrous explosion rocked Black Tom Island.

The Statue of Liberty was illuminated as rockets and shells exploded in the sky for twenty minutes. Then there was a second series of explosions. Buildings on both sides of the Hudson River shook. Windows broke and shards of glass hurtled to the streets below. New Yorkers were thrown from their beds and thousands ran into the streets in confusion, some wearing only their nightclothes.

Fire trucks from all over the city rushed into action, pouring into the streets, then hesitating, unsure of the origins of the terrible explosions. Fires raged throughout the night and chaos reigned as telephones went dead.

The Brooklyn Bridge swayed, terrorizing motorists already frightened by their shattered windshields. People as far south as Philadelphia, Pennsylvania, believed there had been an earthquake.

By dawn, thousands were lining the shorelines watching and waiting for word.

Thirteen massive warehouses filled with weapons and ammunition had been destroyed by German saboteurs. Six piers, and hundreds of railroad cars and barges, were now charred ruins. The blast left a hole that was below sea level. Water seeped in, creating an eerie wreckage-strewn pond. Newspapers ran the following headlines:

CITY IS TERROR STRICKEN
GREAT PART OF POPULATION RUSHES TO STREETS,
MANY IN NIGHT ATTIRE, SEEKING SAFETY
RIVER BRIDGES TREMBLE,
ALL POLICE CALLED TO PREVENT LOOTING OF STORES

Three men and a child were killed (the child died having been thrown from his crib). The damage was estimated in the millions.

The sabotage on Black Tom Island shocked the nation.

The disaster at Black Tom Island was a shocking blow. But it was not an isolated incident. In subsequent years, it would be learned that there had been two hundred acts of sabotage committed on United States property prior to America's entry into World War I.

DRAFT DODGERS

The number of men needed when the United States entered World War I was enormous. To meet that need, President Woodrow Wilson turned to the draft. The draft (sometimes called conscription) is the forced recruitment of men into the military. According to the Selective Service Act of 1917, men between the ages of 21 and 30 were eligible to be drafted and therefore were required to register. In previous years, draftees were allowed to pay someone to go in their place, or pay money to avoid service. These practices were not permitted during World War I.

There were those in government who claimed that as many as 300,000 draft dodgers were avoiding service in the armed forces. (Others strongly believed this was an exaggeration.) There was as much alarm over draft dodgers as there was over spies and saboteurs. The Bureau of Investigation was responsible for insuring that the Selective Service laws were being obeyed. Because of the war, the bureau's responsibilities had increased. By 1918, the number of agents in the bureau had grown from 300 to 400. Some Americans, however, feared that that wasn't enough. They believed that law enforcement agencies didn't have the manpower necessary to handle the crises brought on by the war. Vigilante groups, made up of Americans who wanted to take the law into their own hands, sprang up around the country. There was a growing public hysteria. People began reporting their neighbors for voicing what they considered unpatriotic sentiments. Innocent people were threatened by newly formed committees that questioned their loyalty to America.

The largest of these vigilante groups was the American Protective League (APL). Membership in this all-volunteer organization was eventually estimated at 250,000. There were APL chapters in every major city. The APL leadership offered its services to the Justice Department. The head of the Bureau of Investigation and the attorney general accepted its offer. The APL members were issued official-looking badges that read:

THE AMERICAN PROTECTIVE LEAGUE, AUXILIARY TO THE U.S. DEPARTMENT OF JUSTICE.

Bureau agents, along with badge-bearing APL members, swarmed into major cities in search of those who sought to avoid military service. In New York, more than 60,000 men were rounded up; in Chicago, 27,000. Anyone who was thought to be a draft dodger was whisked off the street. Men were dragged from movie theaters, restaurants, trains, and hotel rooms. Cars were halted and drivers ordered out. Bureau agents and APL volunteers roamed the streets on foot and by car, arresting anyone who was unable to produce a draft card. People were herded like cattle and forced to stand for hours without being able to phone for help. Many had to spend the night in jail.

The overwhelming majority of those picked up turned out to be innocent: 199 out of every 200 arrested. Most of them were either too young, too old, or too sick to be drafted. Others had simply left their draft cards at home.

The decision to allow the APL to act as agents of the United States government resulted in some of the most flagrant violations of civil liberties in American history.

RADICALS AND EXTREMISTS

Internal unrest and upheaval did not disappear after World War I. In 1919, the year after the war ended, there were over 3,600 strikes nationwide. Four million workers refused to go to work until they got more pay and better working conditions. Some, however, were participating in the strikes because they also wanted to change the government of the United States. They wanted to change it from a democracy with a capitalist economic system to a communist society. Some believed that this change could be achieved within the democratic process. But others believed that the change could only take place if there was a revolution in the United States and the government was forcibly overthrown.

In a capitalist system, the land and factories are owned by individuals and private companies. People can decide what jobs they want to pursue and how they want to spend their money. Companies decide what products they will make and what price they will charge. There is open competition among companies in a free market.

In a communist system, the land and factories are owned by the government. In countries that become communist, businesses and factories that were previously owned by individuals are "nationalized." This means that the companies are taken over by the government. Private ownership is eliminated and government control is put in its place. Communists believe that the workers in capitalist countries are taken advantage of by the rich, those who own and control the factories, industries, and businesses.

In 1917, a communist revolution had overthrown the Czarist government of Russia. The Russian communists supported workers who wanted to revolt in other countries. Communist uprisings occurred in a number of European countries. Most Americans were opposed to communism and feared that America might be the next target. Communists were accused of encouraging strikes, unrest, violence, and revolution in the United States.

THE "PALMER RAIDS"

On June 2, 1919, an unidentified group of radicals detonated bombs destined for government officials in twelve cities. One of those bombs was meant for Attorney General A. Mitchell Palmer, who escaped unhurt. The front of Palmer's house was destroyed, however, and the bomb thrower was killed in the explosion. A flier attacking capitalism was found in the debris.

Congress had been pressuring the Justice Department to do something about communists and others whom the government viewed as extremists. Attorney General Palmer told Congress he had certain information that there would soon be an "attempt to rise up and destroy the government." Palmer moved to put an end to the violence and protect the government from those who were seeking to destroy it.

A couple of weeks after the bombing, the Justice Department had an all-day meeting at which a strategy was developed. The plan was a nationwide roundup of aliens who were considered radical by the government. (Aliens are people who live in a country they were not born in and where they have not obtained citizenship.)

The Justice Department decided to take action against people who were not citizens of the United States, for two reasons. One, unlike American citizens, aliens could be legally deported if they believed in political violence or belonged to an organization that did. Deportation — removing them from the United States — was Palmer's goal.

The second reason, Palmer claimed, was that "the results of investigations made by this department into the ultraradical movement . . . of the last year has clearly indicated that fully 90% of the . . . agitation is traceable to aliens."

Palmer's bold plan was one of the most extraordinary operations in American history. It was also one of the most embarrassing. On the night of January 2, 1920, agents of the Bureau of Investigation working with local police raided meeting halls, tearing down doors, smashing furniture, and confiscating pamphlets. In a massive nationwide dragnet, more than ten thousand people were arrested in thirty-three cities.

The raids displayed, however, a nearly total disregard for basic human rights. The vast majority of arrests were made without warrants. Many of those arrested didn't speak English and, therefore, didn't understand what was happening to them. There were reports that many of them had been beaten. Although some foreigners were involved in the violence of the early 1900s, most of those caught in the "Palmer Raids" were not guilty of any violation of the law. Of the more than ten thousand

The "Palmer Raids" were directed against alien radicals.

people arrested, only five hundred and fifty-six were eventually deported.

Initially, the response to the raids was enthusiastic, especially in the press. *The New York Times* editorialized: "If any of us . . . have ever doubted the . . . intelligence of the Department of Justice in hunting down the enemies of the United States, the questioners and doubters now have cause to approve and applaud."

But gradually, as the details of the raids became known, the "Palmer Raids" began to come under harsh criticism.

The National Civil Liberties Bureau (which was to be renamed the American Civil Liberties Union) protested the beating of prisoners in New York City. Government officials began to publicly question the tactics used. A group of highly respected law professors wrote a report criticizing the brutality employed and the conditions of the jails in which those arrested were kept. The *Report Upon the Illegal Practices of the United States Department of Justice* began: "For more than six months, we, the undersigned lawyers, whose sworn duty it is to uphold the Constitution and Laws of the United States, have seen with growing apprehension the continued violation of that Constitution and breaking of those laws by the Department of Justice of the United States government." In early 1921, a Senate investigation showed that most of the accusations against the raids were true.

In the months following the raids, Palmer was attacked for his behavior. He remained, however, unrepentant. "I apologize for nothing that the Department of Justice has done in this matter. I glory in it."

The "Palmer Raids" did weaken communist and other extreme left-wing groups in the United States. However, the raids were an embarrassment to the still-young Bureau of Investigation and those directly responsible. The man who planned and carried out the raids was a young, ambitious bureau assistant named J. Edgar Hoover.

J. Edgar Hoover, early in his FBI career

The years following the "Palmer Raids" continued to be embarrassing ones for the government. The administration of President Warren G. Harding proved to be notoriously corrupt and the Bureau of Investigation deteriorated even further.

It wasn't until 1924, when Harlan Fiske Stone was named attorney general, that things began to change. Stone knew the bureau was filled with agents who had been given jobs as favors. Many were incompetent, some outright crooks. Stone needed someone who could clean up the bureau.

On May 10, 1924, Attorney General Stone named 29-year-old J. Edgar Hoover Acting Director of the Bureau of Investigation.

J. Edgar Hoover and parents, Annie and Dickerson Hoover

CHAPTER TWO

★

"SPEED"

"From the day he entered the Department, certain things marked Hoover apart from scores of other young law clerks. He dressed better than most, and a bit on the dandyish side. He had an exceptional capacity for detail work, and he handled small chores with enthusiasm and thoroughness. He constantly sought new responsibilities to shoulder and welcomed chances to work overtime. When he was in conference with an official of his department, his manner was that of a young man who confidently expected to rise."

Journalist Jack Alexander

John Edgar Hoover lived his whole life in Washington, DC. His father, Dickerson Hoover, Sr., worked for the government and his mother, Annie, a forceful woman who believed in discipline, ran the home. They too, were born in the nation's capital. Edgar was born on January 1, 1895. He had a sister, Lillian, who was twelve years older, and a brother Dickerson, Jr., who was fifteen years older. Another sister, Marguerite, died when she was only three. Edgar was especially close to his mother, who adored him, and his brother, whom he grew to idolize.

The Hoovers lived in a two-story white stucco house in a quiet residential neighborhood. There were three bedrooms upstairs, and a dining room, kitchen, and front and rear parlors downstairs. Edgar lived there for the first forty-three years of his life, moving only after his mother died.

Edgar received a proper upbringing. "As a youth I was taught basic

Young Hoover

The house where Hoover grew up and lived until the age of forty-three

beliefs. For instance, I was taught that no book was ever to be placed above the Bible. Children in my youth were taught the code of the American flag, and to defend it against any manner of desecration, as a symbol of life, liberty, and justice," Hoover recalled years later.

He sang in the church choir and went to an elementary school a block away. But later, his mother insisted he travel the three miles to Washington's Central High School because it was thought to be the best in the city. He spent most of his time on schoolwork, never participating in the teenage drinking, gambling, and card playing that went on all around him. He preferred family to friends and was a bright and serious student. His niece and neighbor, Mrs. Margaret Fennell, remembers her uncle as someone with a purpose: "I think that early in his career, J. E. decided that he was going to achieve something big and I don't think he let himself be distracted from that."

Edgar excelled in schoolwork, especially math. But history was his favorite subject and he became interested in criminals and their crimes. He liked to argue and joined the debate society, where he earned a reputation as a tough opponent. His debating team was undefeated.

His mother called him Edgar, his cousins J. E., but his friends nicknamed him "Speed." Some say it was because of the rapid way he carried groceries for people to earn extra money. Others say it was because of his machine-gunlike manner of speaking. (In order to overcome an early stuttering problem, he spent hours practicing in front of his bedroom mirror.)

In 1913, when he was 18, he graduated from Central High School after earning honors as class valedictorian. He took a job as a messenger and file clerk at the Library of Congress, where he learned their complex card-indexing system while cataloging new books as they came in. He worked there for four years while going to law school at George Washington University in the evenings. Edgar had wanted to go to the University of Virginia, where he had been awarded a scholarship, but the expense of living away from home was more than the family could afford. In July, 1917, he received his law degree and took a job as a clerk in the Justice Department.

It was quite natural for him to work in the government. His grandfather and father did, and Dickerson, Jr., worked next door in the Commerce Department.

Edgar worked hard, bringing work home almost every evening. He was determined, dedicated, and detail-oriented. He impressed his supervisors as an ambitious young man with a bright future. His next seven years in the Justice Department would see him rise steadily, earning him promotion after promotion.

HOOVER'S EARLY CAREER

Only three months after taking his first job in the Justice Department, Hoover had been given his first promotion. His superiors were impressed with his work habits and confident attitude.

In 1917, the twenty-two-year-old Hoover had been placed in charge of a unit of the department's enemy alien registration section. His responsibilities included reviewing the wartime cases of aliens who were considered dangerous. He then recommended a course of action: parole, confinement within the United States, or deportation. Hoover was driven by a desire to do a good job, but also by his anger at what he considered the anti-American attitude of most aliens. After only two years on the job, Hoover was considered the Justice Department's expert on aliens.

In August, 1919, Attorney General Palmer appointed Hoover head of another new division, the General Intelligence Division, known as the GID. Its task was to research groups whose political views the government considered too radical and, therefore, dangerous.

Using the experience he gained as a clerk in the Library of Congress, Hoover created an index of 100,000 individuals who were considered political extremists. Within a few months, the list had grown to 200,000 and, by the third year, 450,000. Not content with this, Hoover had files created on 60,000 people he considered the most dangerous. The GID quickly became the largest division within the Bureau of Investigation.

Hoover also conducted what he considered a thorough study of communism. He concluded that communists throughout the world were part of a conspiracy directed by the government of the Soviet Union. Hoover was convinced that the communists were nothing more than criminals. "Communism," he wrote, "is the most evil, monstrous conspiracy since time began." His studies established him as the government's number one authority on communism.

Attorney General Palmer had read Hoover's studies before he placed him in charge of his war on radicals and communists. Hoover's World

War I experience dealing with undesirable aliens had convinced him to give Hoover full responsibility for planning the "Palmer Raids."

THE DIRECTOR

In August, 1921, one year after the "Palmer Raids," Hoover was named assistant director of the Bureau of Investigation. Three years later, in 1924, he was named acting director by newly appointed Attorney General Stone. Stone stressed that Hoover must make sure the bureau stopped spending its time investigating political activities. Stone wanted the bureau to investigate only actual violations of federal law.

Hoover assured Attorney General Stone that he agreed. "Our bureau carries on no investigations of matters that are not contrary to federal statutes," the newly appointed acting director announced.

Stone's appointment of Hoover was criticized by some on the grounds that Hoover was too young. The attorney general, however, looked on this as a plus, rather than a minus: "Everyone says he's too young, but maybe that's his asset. Apparently he hasn't learned to be afraid of the politicians, and I believe he would set up a group of young men as investigators and infuse them with a will to operate independent of congressional and political pressure."

Hoover did not disappoint the attorney general. He was taking over at a time when the bureau's integrity was being widely questioned. But he was determined to improve that image. He knew just what was wrong with the bureau and precisely what he was going to do about it.

Working under the attorney general's direct supervision, Hoover set about rebuilding the bureau. Seven months later, he was named permanent director. His efforts in those first few months, and in the months to come, laid the foundation for today's FBI.

The new director of the bureau

CHAPTER THREE

★

HOOVER BUILDS THE BUREAU

"This Bureau cannot afford to have a public scandal visited upon it in the view of the all too numerous attacks made . . . during the past few years. I do not want this Bureau to be referred to in terms I have frequently heard used against other government agencies."

J. Edgar Hoover

Hoover decided to focus on the areas that needed improvement most urgently. There were many, and he was wise in his choices and adept at implementing his plans. From the beginning, he had a nearly complete vision of how the new FBI would function. He attacked each area relentlessly, making it clear to those around him that he would accept nothing less than perfection. He pursued his goals with an air of confidence that was quickly conveyed to those around him. In the area of organization — a large part of making any government bureau function — he was a genius.

The areas that Hoover considered most important were upgrading personnel and instituting proper training procedures, shaping an efficient and closely managed department, organizing and systematizing the storage and retrieval of information, creating a close working relationship with local law enforcement agencies, and launching programs that would educate the public as to the functions of what he envisioned as the nation's premier, scientific crime-fighting force.

THE NEW FBI AGENT

Hoover put an end to the unofficial bureau policy of giving jobs as a reward for political favors. Agents who had criminal records or whose characters were in question were fired. Those not fired were retrained. Others were driven out by a tactic Hoover would use throughout his reign: the short-notice transfer (referred to by insiders as "on the bicycle"). The unwanted agent would be ordered to pack his bags and report immediately to a new post. It wasn't long before he received his next notice, and on and on, until he resigned. Others quit without provocation, unwilling to work under the new, strict guidelines being issued from Washington.

The new director insisted that the bureau have its own entrance exam; one that was tougher than the civil service exam they had been using. Salaries were increased and benefits upgraded. Within a few years, becoming an FBI agent was considered prestigious.

Citizens of the United States who were male, between the ages of twenty-five and forty, had 20/20 vision, good hearing, and good health were eligible to apply. Those with law or accounting degrees were given preference. Hoover believed that the federal government had lost too many cases because the evidence had not been gathered and presented in a professional manner. Having agents with the proper education would, he hoped, lead to more convictions in court. (Exceptions were made, especially in the 1940s when World War II necessitated an increase in the number of agents. To meet this requirement, Hoover relaxed the standards.)

Hoover preferred applicants who weren't "fresh out of college." He believed that those who were doing postgraduate work, or had been working in a job that was applicable to bureau work, would be more mature, and therefore better agents.

Applicants were interviewed by the FBI agent in charge of the field office nearest their homes. The agent emphasized the tedious reality, not the glamour, of the life of an FBI agent: Little time was spent tracking down dangerous criminals, guns blazing. Being an FBI agent meant countless hours of reading and analyzing documents, interviewing witnesses, collecting evidence for the lab, and perhaps most time-consuming, writing reports.

After the written exam, the FBI agent sent a report to Washington. Potential agents were then investigated by the FBI. Teachers, employers, fellow workers, family, and neighbors were interviewed as to the applicant's character, work habits, and personal life. Candidates who were accepted were then invited to attend a sixteen-week FBI training course in and around Washington, DC.

The course was divided into classroom work and practical application. Classes were given in proper investigative techniques, the FBI's responsibilities under the law, fingerprint identification, preservation of evidence at the crime scene, and report writing.

(Agents are now trained at the U.S. Marine base in Quantico, Virginia, forty miles south of Washington. These new recruits are taught self-defense techniques and given rigorous physical conditioning.

There is extensive training in the proper use of firearms. Basics, like the correct way to squeeze a trigger or how to take apart, clean, and reassemble a pistol, are drilled. The potential agent is trained to be an expert shot using revolvers, rifles, shotguns, and submachine guns. He is also taught how to launch tear gas accurately.)

In 1946, a new electronic firing range was unveiled. Life-size and life-like targets (photos of notorious gangsters were reproduced on the sil-

Once director, Hoover insisted on the proper training of FBI agents in all areas, including the use of weapons.

houettes) appeared suddenly in a variety of positions: surrendering or shooting, from behind a barricade or out in the open. The candidates made split-second decisions whether or not to shoot. Hasty action could mean killing someone about to surrender, but hesitation could result in a dead FBI agent. The time it took a recruit to make those decisions was electronically calculated.

The candidates learn to fire their weapons from a variety of positions: standing, kneeling, sitting, and lying flat. They are taught never to fire while running and to shoot only in self-defense. They are trained, however, to shoot to kill.

At the U.S. Marine base in Quantico, the classroom lessons are applied to practical situations. Crime conditions — hit-and-runs or robberies, for example — are simulated. The recruits learn how to take photographs at the scene of a crime, lift fingerprints, make plaster casts of tire tracks, judge the speed of a car from its skid marks, follow proper surveillance techniques, and search a crime scene thoroughly to gather evidence to be sent to the FBI lab for analysis. The trainees practice interviewing witnesses and appearing as witnesses at mock trials.

In the 1930s and 1940s, FBI training procedures were looked upon by those in government and law enforcement as the best in the country. They helped build the reputation of the FBI agent as a member of an elite organization.

RULES AND REGULATIONS

When the twenty-nine-year-old Hoover became director, he was in charge of approximately 650 employees. Of this number, 441 agents carried on the investigative work from FBI field offices throughout the United States. The others were support personnel including typists, file clerks, and laboratory technicians. All were informed that they would be expected to live up to a set of high standards. Drinking, on or off the

Agents study results of a practice session at the shooting range.

job, was prohibited. Unseemly behavior would not be tolerated. Coffee breaks were out, and personal property was not allowed at office desks. New *Rules and Regulations and Instructions* manuals were issued. They spelled out the proper procedures to follow when investigating and reporting a federal crime. The manual was revised twice within the next three years.

Uniform filing and reporting systems were installed in all field offices. This allowed agents to be transferred easily from one office to another.

Hoover established a strong chain of command, creating six separate divisions, each with clearly defined areas of responsibility.

He announced a system of periodic unannounced field visits. Inspectors from the Internal Inspection Division visited each office at least once a year. Agents who performed well were given merit points. Those who didn't, received demerits. Acquiring enough merit points could result in a promotion or raise in pay. Enough demerits could lead to a transfer to an unpopular location or, finally, to dismissal.

Bureau agents were encouraged to report directly to Hoover any rule violations by other employees. Agents were advised that they were, technically, on duty twenty-four hours a day. Cars were to be kept bright and shiny and agents were responsible for maintaining their personal appearance. "I want the public to look upon the bureau as a group of gentlemen," Hoover stated. "And if the men here engaged can't conduct themselves in office as such, I will dismiss them." Before too long, bureau agents were considered men of goodwill and superior character.

FINGERPRINTS

The Bertillon system was the first method of criminal identification. It used a complex combination of body measurements (such as the size of the head or the length of the left forearm and index finger) to identify people. At the time, it was thought that no two people could have the same appearance and the same measurements. By 1924, there were 200,000 Bertillon files stored in the Justice Department.

Hoover considered the Bertillon system obsolete and scrapped it.

In 1924, Congress had decided that all fingerprint records should be managed by the FBI and centrally located in Washington, DC. Since no two fingerprints are the same, fingerprinting is considered a better system than the Bertillon. The Department of Justice's fingerprint files were to be combined with those of the International Association of Chiefs of Police. Conditions in the bureau at the time were chaotic and there was

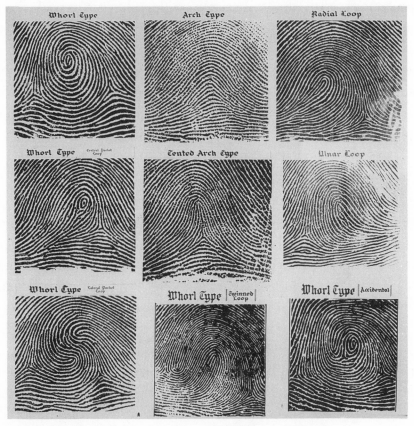

Hoover supported the use of fingerprints to identify criminals.

no money set aside for this task. As a result, 810,188 sets of prints sat in storage for months.

Hoover went to Congress and obtained the necessary funds to consolidate all the fingerprint records. In June, 1930, Congress formally authorized the creation of a Division of Identification and Information within the bureau. This efficient, well-organized division helped identify fugitives once they were arrested. Before, a fugitive could easily escape detection simply by using an alias.

To have your fingerprints on file with the FBI became a popular and patriotic thing to do in the 1930s. Tour guides told visitors of the benefits: It could help you if you got amnesia or were injured and couldn't be identified. A card with a single fingerprint was given as a souvenir.

The Division of Identification and Information was crafted by Hoover into an internationally known crime-fighting resource. By the mid-1970s the files were growing at the rate of 3,000 sets a day. By 1986, the FBI had amassed fingerprints of over 60 million people.

SCIENTIFIC CRIME FIGHTING

In 1932, Hoover created the FBI's Criminal Laboratory. Its facilities were available to local police across the nation as well as agents in the field. (Thirty percent of the examinations conducted by the lab were for outside agencies.) The lab could analyze an incredible variety of evidence. A discarded cigarette butt or a thread from a coat was often enough to identify a suspect. A bullet could provide enough information to save a case. A speck of paint or fragments from a broken headlight might identify the make and model of a getaway car. In kidnapping cases, paper could be analyzed, typewriters traced, and handwriting identified (sometimes revealing whether the writer of the note had been forced to write it). A lipstick stain could begin a trail that led from manufacturer to store to customer to suspect.

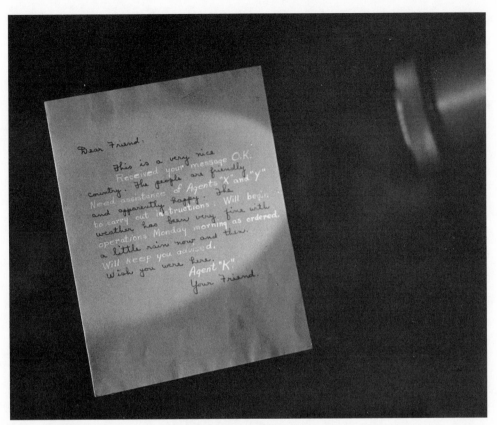

Hoover's FBI led the way in applying science to crime solving. The FBI Laboratory demonstrates how to use ultraviolet light to reveal hidden messages.

FLIGHT No. 629

One well-known FBI case illustrates the benefits of the centrally coordinated, scientific organization Hoover had created. The case unfolded 5,700 feet above the city of Denver, Colorado, on the night of November 1, 1955.

When United Airlines flight No. 629 crashed eleven minutes after takeoff, the Civil Aeronautics Board requested the FBI's assistance.

The FBI's Disaster Squad, which makes its resources available to help identify victims of airplane crashes and other accidents, was immediately sent to the scene.

The FBI was able to identify twenty-one of the forty-four people who were aboard the plane (nine had already been identified) by tracing their fingerprints through the Division of Identification and Information. (Some had served in the military, some worked for the government, and others had their prints on file because they had recently applied for U.S. citizenship.)

Agent Roy Moore, later to become well-known as one of the bureau's top investigators, was the assistant in charge of the FBI's Denver field office. He supervised the investigation.

A grid was set up at a warehouse at the airport. The wreckage covered a two-mile area. The plane's shell could be constructed except for a jagged hole in the cargo area.

FBI lab personnel took the pieces of evidence back to Washington where they were analyzed.

Pieces of metal were found that were clean on one side but burned on the other. Some bits of metal had been driven through the soles of shoes, and pieces of brass from luggage were found embedded in the steel.

Five fragments of sheet metal that could not be identified as part of the plane or its cargo were discovered. The fragments were badly burned and coated with chemicals associated with the explosion of dynamite. This all pointed to a bomb blast. By the end of the week, nearly a hundred agents were tracking down leads.

One passenger's luggage was not recovered, except for a few tiny pieces. The luggage compartment was where the blast was thought to have occurred. If there had been a bomb in that suitcase, it would explain why the luggage had disintegrated.

Agents conducted a thorough investigation of all thirty-nine passengers and five crew members. Their findings led them to Jack Gilbert Graham, whose mother had been on the flight.

Graham, twenty-three, had filled out insurance policies at the airport listing himself as his mother's beneficiary. He had helped his mother with her luggage before she boarded the plane. Graham, however, denied knowing anything about the crash.

Agents also discovered that Graham was entitled to half of the $50,000 his mother left in her will. And that wasn't all. While interviewing his wife, they learned that he had bought his mother a going-away present. Graham hadn't mentioned that to the FBI. They learned that he had bought a timing device the week before and, while searching his home, they found copper wire in a shirt pocket.

On November 14, two weeks after the crash, Graham confessed to FBI agent Moore. He had indeed blown up the plane and killed his mother and all those aboard for the insurance money and the money left in the will.

A jury deliberated a little over an hour before convicting Graham of first degree murder. On January 11, 1957, Jack Graham was put to death in the gas chamber.

THE FBI NATIONAL ACADEMY:
"A UNIVERSITY OF LAW ENFORCEMENT"

In 1935, to create a closer working relationship with local law enforcement agencies, Hoover launched another major innovation: the FBI Police Training School.

The idea of a school for police and law enforcement officers from around the country had been proposed by Hoover at a crime conference held the year before. The idea was well received. Hoover believed that teaching modern criminology, such as the FBI itself used, to local law enforcement agencies was a key to combating criminals.

The FBI National Academy was moved to the Marine base in Quantico, Virginia, where it remains today.

The FBI National Academy (as it was renamed in 1945) was an important part of Hoover's plan for the new bureau. He envisioned having the FBI create scientific crime-fighting resources at the FBI and then teach other lawmen how to use them.

On July 29, 1935, the first class of twenty-three officers began the twelve-week course (there were two sessions each year). When the courses first began, the teaching was done in downtown Washington. In the coming two decades, more than 3,000 officers graduated from the National Academy, which was eventually located at the FBI's own training facilities at Quantico, Virginia.

Candidates were selected by a process that involved local police chiefs and the FBI agents in charge of the regional field office in their areas. (Since 1962, law enforcement personnel from friendly foreign countries have also attended.)

Experienced FBI agents, along with outside specialists, taught proper police procedure, administration methods, investigative techniques, firearms use, modern crime fighting, and the latest advances in scientific criminology.

Graduating from the National Academy gave a police officer a better chance for career advancement. But more important, it helped Hoover create a cooperative relationship between the FBI agent in the field and the local police.

THE *MODUS OPERANDI* FILE

Modus operandi is a Latin phrase meaning "method of operating." It is mostly used to describe criminal activity. A person's *modus operandi* (or MO) is made up of things a particular criminal typically does when committing crimes: whether or not he uses force, whether she works alone, or whether he is usually armed.

The file notes the techniques used by known criminals. These characteristics are often particular enough to identify those criminals. The *modus operandi* file can be of great value in cases where there are no witnesses or where the witnesses are unable to identify suspects from photographs.

THE TEN MOST WANTED LIST

The FBI's list of the Ten Most Wanted criminals was popularized by Hoover beginning in 1950. It was an effective tool and an immediate success. Almost every newspaper in the country ran photographs of the Ten Most Wanted fugitives. Frequently criminals were picked up because someone spotted them in a newspaper, magazine, or on a post office wall. One magazine feature alone resulted in the arrest of three of the top ten. Hundreds of criminals were found because of the list.

The FBI still maintains a list of the Ten Most Wanted fugitives. They are selected according to "past criminal record, the threat posed to the community, the seriousness of the crime for which the fugitive is sought, and whether nationwide publicity is likely to assist in apprehension."

Although Hoover was considered young for the job, he acted older than his years. He was an excellent administrator and a tireless worker. He went over paperwork every night after dinner in his room and gave his full attention to the smallest detail. He drove the people working under him as hard as he drove himself.

As director, Hoover had successfully introduced scientific law enforcement to the American public. The FBI would, in years to come, be synonymous with the precise, skilled, painstaking and, in some cases, near magical analysis of clues and evidence.

J. Edgar Hoover had taken the FBI from its lowest point and transformed it into one of the most highly regarded divisions in the government. Although there were critics, they were in the minority.

Hoover instituted the Ten Most Wanted list as a way to get the public involved in the FBI's fight against crime.

Destroying beer barrels during Prohibition

CHAPTER FOUR

★

G-MEN, GANGSTERS, KILLERS, AND KIDNAPPERS

"Well, they had Dillinger surrounded and was all ready to shoot him when he came out, but another bunch of folks came out ahead, so they just shot them instead. Dillinger is going to accidentally get with some innocent bystanders some time, then he will get shot."

Humorist Will Rogers

The Eighteenth Amendment, which was one of the least obeyed laws in American history, had been passed by Congress and became the law of the land in 1919. This amendment to the Constitution stated that: "the manufacture, sale, or transportation of intoxicating liquors within . . . the United States . . . is hereby prohibited." This was the beginning of the period known as Prohibition, an era marked by widespread disregard for the law and spectacular crimes. Criminals across the country, realizing there were fortunes to be made, jumped on the bootlegging bandwagon. (A bootlegger was someone who sold liquor illegally. The term originated during the Civil War, when peddlers hid whiskey bottles in their bootlegs.) Congress gave the Treasury Department federal responsibility for enforcing this law.

During Prohibition, which ended in 1933 when the law was withdrawn, bootlegging grew and became organized. In Chicago, New York, Detroit, Boston, and other cities, ruthless gangsters ruled large areas.

47

Overlords like Al Capone, "Legs" Diamond, "Dutch" Schultz, and Louis "Lepke" Buchalter controlled vast empires with laws of their own. And when these laws were violated they saw to it that their own brand of "justice" was done. City streets became the scenes of daytime murders, complete with screeching tires and bullet-spewing machine guns.

Gangland wars erupted over disputed boundaries and, on February 14, 1929, the violence peaked. Four gangsters, dressed as policemen, gunned down seven rival gang members. That execution became known as the St. Valentine's Day Massacre.

THE DEPRESSION

On October 24, 1929, "Black Thursday," the stock market crashed. Stock values declined steadily for three years. This marked the beginning of the period in America known as the Depression.

The 1930s were a time of widespread unemployment and profound poverty. Millions lost their jobs, their savings, and their homes. Those who did work made very little. In Manhattan, factories — called sweatshops — paid a dollar a day.

By 1933, 9,000 banks had been forced to close their doors. Many people lost their life savings. The economy grew worse almost every month. By 1935, there were 13 million unemployed — 25 percent of the population. Seventeen thousand people shined shoes for a living in New York City.

The hungry ransacked garbage dumps looking for food and ate dog meat when all else failed. Many depended on the government for food. Some died of disease resulting from malnutrition. Farms were being taken over by the banks because people couldn't afford to pay their mortgages. The combination of drought and wind storms turned the Midwest into a "dust bowl." People lived in makeshift shacks that utilized flattened tin cans and old crates. "Brother Can You Spare a Dime?" was a popular song, and desperation was a way of life for many.

A breadline during the Depression

KILLERS

During the last years of Prohibition and the start of the Depression, violence and crime spread across the country. Coldhearted killers and brazen bank robbers plagued the Midwest. Criminals drove fast cars and used high-powered rifles and machine guns. (Automobiles gave criminals mobility and contributed significantly to the growth of crime.) Often the criminals were better armed than the police. Banks were robbed in one state and the gang hid out in another. Crime had become a national, not a local, problem. The American public, fed by almost constant coverage in the press, had become fascinated by celebrity criminals. The public had lost confidence in the government's ability to stop the wave of violence.

Congress passed new laws to help the FBI rid the country of these criminals. Taking a kidnapped person from one state to another became a federal offense. The Federal Extortion Act allowed the government to put the writer of a threatening letter in prison for as long as twenty years. The Federal Bank Robbery Act protected all national banks and banks whose deposits were insured by the government. These crime bills gave FBI agents more power and expanded their jurisdiction. By 1934, the FBI was enforcing more than a hundred federal statutes.

The new laws not only gave FBI agents more responsibility, they also gave them more protection. Killing or assaulting a federal officer now carried stiff penalties. Agents, for the first time, had the authority to carry guns, guns that were needed as they set out to confront a dangerous cast of characters.

"PRETTY BOY" FLOYD: Charles Arthur Floyd terrorized the Southwest in the 1930s, killing ten people, including five policemen.

His first recorded crime was stealing $350 in pennies from the post office when he was 18. An eyewitness to his first major crime described him as having a "pretty face." The description led to his arrest and he was given a five-year sentence.

After serving a little over a year, "Pretty Boy" Floyd was released, only to be rearrested numerous times. On his way to prison to serve a 10- to 25-year sentence for bank robbery, he escaped through a train window. He was never put behind bars again.

The FBI finally caught up with him on an Ohio farm in 1934. When he attempted to escape, he was killed.

"BABY FACE" NELSON: Nelson was born Lester Gillis. He was one of the few gangsters of this era who went out of his way to kill. He stole cars and robbed gas stations, later graduating to banks. A bank guard described him as "a young man with a baby face." Nelson hated the name, but it stuck.

Nelson's reputation for killing for pleasure helped earn him the status of "Public Enemy No. 1." On November 27, 1934, two FBI agents were shot and died after mortally wounding "Baby Face" in a blazing gun battle.

"MA" BARKER: Her real first name was Arizona, but she preferred Kate. She and her four sons — Herman, Lloyd, Arthur "Dock," and Fred — robbed banks, kidnapped businessmen, and killed policemen in the late 1920s and early 1930s.

The Barkers were dirt-poor all their lives. The boys began by committing petty crimes, but were soon stealing cars. Before long, "Ma" became head of the gang.

In 1927, Herman had been caught in the act of robbing a bank. Unwilling to surrender, he killed a policeman, but was blinded by a bullet during the shoot-out. With the police closing in, Herman killed himself with one pistol shot to the head.

Clockwise from top, right: "Ma" and "Pa" Barker; "Pretty Boy" Floyd; "Baby Face" Nelson

In 1931, Lloyd was sentenced to twenty-five years in Leavenworth Federal Penitentiary in Kansas for mail robbery. Twenty-two years later, when he was fifty-one, he was released. He was later murdered by his wife, who claimed he was going to kill her and the children.

"Dock" was given a life sentence for killing a night watchman. In 1932, he was given a banishment parole, which meant he had to leave the state of Oklahoma. Thanks to the efficiency of the FBI's fingerprint file, he was later identified in a kidnapping case. In 1935, he was sentenced to life imprisonment again and was subsequently killed while making an escape.

By 1933, "Ma" had earned a reputation, and criminals, such as Alvin "Old Creepy" Karpis, sought her out in hopes of joining forces with her. "Ma" was the brains behind the operation. She cased the banks, planned the robberies, and drew up the getaway routes. Fred, who had spent five years in reform school and had killed a sheriff in Missouri, rarely left her side.

But local and state police, along with the FBI, were closing in. In early 1935, FBI agents surrounded the cottage in Florida where "Ma" and Fred were hiding out. The machine-gun battle between them and the fifteen agents lasted four hours. After the FBI agents had fired 1,500 rounds of ammunition into the house, the shooting from within stopped. When the agents entered the hideout, mother and son were dead. "Ma," a bullet through her heart, still held a machine gun. Fred had been hit eleven times.

ALVIN "OLD CREEPY" KARPIS: Karpis robbed banks and mail trucks, and killed and kidnapped people in the Midwest. Born Francis Alvin Karpoviecz, he, too, began his life of crime with petty robberies: candy stores, groceries, jewelry stores, and gas stations. In 1927, he was sentenced to ten years in the State Reformatory in Hutchinson, Kansas, but escaped after serving two years. A year later he was arrested as a fugitive and returned to prison. There he met Fred Barker and, when he was paroled the next year, was introduced to "Ma" Barker.

"Ma," like her son, took a liking to the coldblooded Karpis. (It was Fred who gave him his nickname because of his chilling stare.) "Ma" taught "Old Creepy" a great deal about crime. Soon they became known as the Barker-Karpis Gang.

After "Ma" Barker's death, Karpis was the last big-name gangster still operating. The FBI intensified its efforts to capture him. They questioned residents of a rooming house where he was thought to be staying. This led to further clues, and Karpis began to feel the heat. He left for Cuba, but the FBI, with Cuban cooperation, continued on his trail. Karpis, however, managed to stay one step away from the dogged and determined federal agents. At one point, the FBI and local police had Karpis cornered but he managed to escape in the confusion surrounding the shoot-out.

With painstaking care, FBI agents were able to trace Karpis's whereabouts because of a purchase of fishing equipment. Bureau agents knew that Karpis had become an avid fisherman. Eyewitnesses of recent robberies had also made agents aware that his appearance had changed.

The FBI manhunt for Karpis was highly publicized. Karpis boldly sent word that he was going to avenge "Ma" Barker's death by killing Hoover, as well as bureau agents in New York, Chicago, and Los Angeles. Finally, agents spotted the car Karpis had been traveling in. Fearing a leak (or so they said) the bureau did not notify local authorities.

Hoover took an all-night flight, accompanied by additional FBI agents, to New Orleans, Louisana. The facts of Karpis's actual arrest, however, are controversial. The official FBI version says that Hoover and twenty agents surrounded the building where Karpis was thought to be. The unsuspecting Karpis surprised them by leaving the building and walking to his car. Hoover then moved in to make the arrest saying, "Put the cuffs on him, boys." (No one, however, had thought to bring handcuffs. Karpis's hands had to be bound with an agent's tie.)

Karpis himself denied that Hoover arrested him. According to Karpis, only after he was in custody did Hoover step in. "The story of Hoover the Hero is false. He didn't lead the attack on me. He hid until I was safely covered by many guns. He waited until he was told the coast was clear. Then he came out to reap the glory. . . . I made Hoover's reputation as a fearless lawman. It's a reputation he doesn't deserve."

In 1936, Karpis was found guilty of kidnapping and was sentenced to life imprisonment.

When he was nearly sixty, Karpis was paroled.

He died in 1979 of an overdose of sleeping pills.

JOHN DILLINGER: John Herbert Dillinger's life of crime began when he was a teenager. Difficult to capture, he was even harder to hold — he broke out of prison twice. Convicted of robbing and beating an Indiana grocer, he spent eleven years in jail. Released in mid-1933, he and his gang robbed banks, stole guns, and released dangerous prisoners from three police stations. They left ten dead and seven wounded.

The FBI was able to enter the case when he drove a stolen vehicle across state lines. Once, agents had him trapped, but he managed to escape with just a leg wound.

Then, in late April 1934, Melvin Purvis, the FBI agent in charge of the Chicago office, received a tip. Dillinger was hiding out in a lodge in Wisconsin.

Hoover wasted no time summoning newsmen to his office. Dillinger, he announced, was about to be captured.

The FBI agents who descended on the lodge didn't ask local law enforcement officials for their help. Instead, they made their way through

John Dillinger

unfamiliar woods, waking the watch dogs that patrolled the grounds. They surrounded the lodge and waited. They were anxious, certain that Dillinger had been alerted by the barking dogs.

It wasn't long before three men came out and got into a car. They didn't see the agents, or hear their warnings to surrender. Convinced that it was Dillinger and his men, the FBI agents opened fire, killing one and seriously wounding the other two. All three, however, were innocent men, local workers who had stopped by the lodge for a drink.

Dillinger had escaped through the back window.

Hoover and the bureau were subjected to heated criticism as soon as the story broke. Many people were taken with Dillinger's ability to outwit the FBI. Hoover made capturing Dillinger, dead or alive, a number one priority. "Stay on Dillinger," he ordered. "Take him alive if you can, but protect yourself." Hoover's boss, Attorney General Homer Cummings, wasn't so thoughtful: "Shoot to kill," he said, "then count to ten."

Newspapers ran Dillinger's picture and readers claimed to have seen him everywhere. (He tried to alter his features by having plastic surgery performed but it didn't work.) Dillinger was so well-known there was even a board game called Dillinger Land.

On June 22, 1934, his thirty-first birthday, the FBI proclaimed John Dillinger "Public Enemy No. 1."

One month later, in Chicago, Dillinger's luck finally ran out. And once again his path would cross that of FBI agent Melvin Purvis.

Purvis had met with Anna Sage, a friend of Dillinger. She was in trouble with the law herself and there was a good chance she was going to be deported. Sage agreed to reveal Dillinger's whereabouts if she were allowed to remain in the country and collect the $15,000 reward.

Anna Sage told Purvis that she and another woman would be going to the movies the next night with Dillinger. She didn't know which movie theater yet, so she would phone just before they left. To make sure there wouldn't be any mistake, she would wear a red dress.

At 5:00 P.M., Anna Sage called the FBI to say it would be the Biograph Theater.

Fifteen FBI agents waited outside. They were stationed at every exit, down the alley, across the street, and around the corner. Purvis, stationed outside the box office, was to light his cigar as a signal that they could close in on Dillinger.

Once again, the FBI did not inform the local Chicago police. The ticket-taker noticed a lot of suspicious looking men hanging around the theater and called the police. The FBI agents hurriedly identified themselves, narrowly avoiding a disaster.

At 10:30 P.M., Dillinger and his two companions, one wearing a red dress, exited the movie theater. Anna Sage fell behind. Dillinger, his senses sharpened after years on the run, knew something was wrong. . . . But it was too late. Dillinger tried to draw his gun, but was gunned down before he got a shot off.

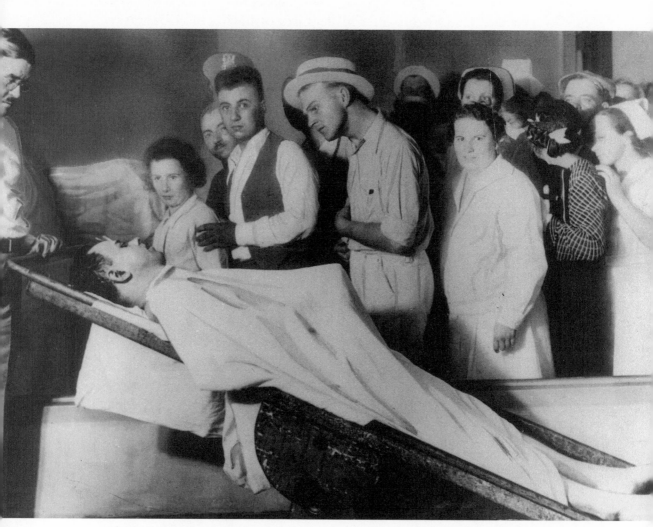

The body of John Dillinger on view at a Chicago morgue

In its own way, the story of what happened to Melvin Purvis tells more about J. Edgar Hoover and the FBI than what happened to John Dillinger.

"Little Mel" Purvis (he wasn't quite five feet seven inches tall, below the FBI's minimum height requirement) became known as "the man who got Dillinger." He was credited not only with masterminding the operation (which he did), but also with firing the shot that killed Dillinger (which he did not). Stories about the cocky little FBI agent appeared in newspapers across the country.

When "Pretty Boy" Floyd was named Public Enemy No. 1 (now that Dillinger had vacated the spot), Purvis led the FBI squad that cornered and killed him in a gun battle.

This was too much for Hoover. He became jealous of the publicity Purvis was getting. Hoover didn't like sharing his press clippings.

J. Edgar Hoover had become a celebrity in his own right. His name popped up regularly in New York City gossip columns. What he wore, where he ate, and with whom were daily news. His hobbies and favorite haunts were tidbits eagerly sought by newspaper reporters and radio personalities.

Hoover had became adept at using publicity to popularize himself and the bureau. *He* was Mr. FBI. Unlike the other nameless and faceless agencies in the federal government, the FBI was symbolized by one man — J. Edgar Hoover. And Hoover wanted to keep it that way.

So Hoover decided to get rid of Mel Purvis. Unable to fire him because of his immense popularity, he decided to harass him till he resigned.

Purvis was sent on fake inspection tours to keep him from talking to reporters. Meanwhile, Hoover did his best to downplay Purvis's role in the Dillinger and "Pretty Boy" Floyd cases. (The officially sanctioned book on the history of the bureau, *The FBI Story*, which was published decades later, does not even list Purvis's name in the index.)

Hoover sent inspectors to the Chicago office to check up on Purvis. They claimed that Purvis spent most of his time on personal business and ignored bureau business; also, that the office was in bad shape. A transfer to a smaller office was recommended. Purvis's denial of the accusations and his charge that the report was a "lie" did him little good.

Only a year after Dillinger's capture, Purvis resigned from the FBI.

Purvis opened his own detective agency. But the word went out from Hoover that no law enforcement agencies were to cooperate with him. Soon he was forced to close it.

Hoover stopped Purvis from getting other jobs, too — one in the motion picture industry and one in racetrack security. Whenever Purvis applied for a job, Hoover made sure a negative report from the bureau went in with his application. (At one point Hoover even changed the record. Purvis's resignation became "termination with extreme prejudice.")

But Purvis still had his fame. His name and face appeared on a nationally known company's breakfast cereal boxes. He was the head of "The Melvin Purvis Law-and-Order Patrol" and was the announcer for a radio program called "The Secrets of the FBI."

Purvis also did ads for cars and razors.

In 1960, a terminally ill Melvin Purvis shot and killed himself.

KIDNAPPERS

In 1931, there were 282 reported kidnappings in the United States. One year later, the most famous kidnapping case in U.S. history unfolded.

Charles Lindbergh was an American hero. The first man to fly solo across the Atlantic Ocean, he was one of the most popular and famous men in the country. In early March, 1932, the news that his twenty-month-old son had been kidnapped from the Lindberghs' Hopewell, New Jersey, home shocked the nation.

Charles and Anne Morrow Lindbergh (*left*) and their baby on his first birthday

At 11:00 P.M. on March 1, Hoover was informed that the Lindberghs' baby had been kidnapped and a ransom note demanding $50,000 had been found at the scene. He gave strict orders that he was to be informed any time, day or night, if something important occurred. He even had a direct line installed from FBI headquarters to his home.

Kidnapping was not a federal offense and the FBI had no jurisdiction in the case. But the Lindbergh kidnapping was to become the major news story of the time and the publicity-conscious Hoover wasted no time offering his unofficial assistance.

Lindbergh and his wife refused to see Hoover when he arrived at their home three days after the kidnapping. The head of the New Jersey State police, Superintendent H. Norman Schwarzkopf (father of General H. Norman Schwarzkopf, who led the forces in the Persian Gulf War) also turned down Hoover's offer to help. Local authorities, already fighting among themselves in the case, considered the federal agents "glory hunters."

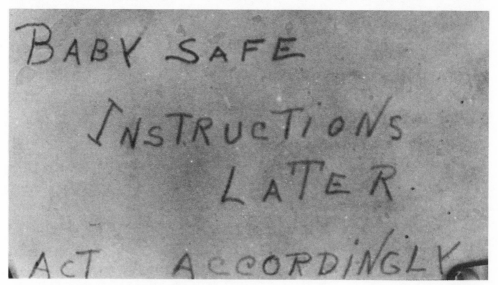

A note from the kidnapper

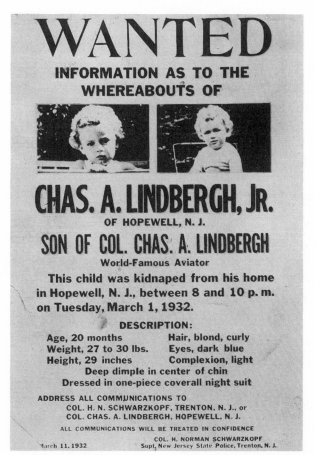

WANTED

INFORMATION AS TO THE WHEREABOUTS OF

CHAS. A. LINDBERGH, JR.
OF HOPEWELL, N. J.
SON OF COL. CHAS. A. LINDBERGH
World-Famous Aviator

This child was kidnaped from his home in Hopewell, N. J., between 8 and 10 p. m. on Tuesday, March 1, 1932.

DESCRIPTION:

Age, 20 months	Hair, blond, curly
Weight, 27 to 30 lbs.	Eyes, dark blue
Height, 29 inches	Complexion, light

Deep dimple in center of chin
Dressed in one-piece coverall night suit

ADDRESS ALL COMMUNICATIONS TO
COL. H. N. SCHWARZKOPF, TRENTON, N. J., or
COL. CHAS. A. LINDBERGH, HOPEWELL, N. J.

ALL COMMUNICATIONS WILL BE TREATED IN CONFIDENCE

COL. H. NORMAN SCHWARZKOPF
March 11, 1932   Supt, New Jersey State Police, Trenton, N. J.

The Lindbergh kidnapping is one of the most notorious crimes of the century.

Hoover went forward anyway. He set up a twenty-man "Lindbergh Squad" and worked with cooperative writers who produced stories for the press. The "Lindbergh Squad" was ordered to stay on the case and follow every lead, despite the refusal of local police to share any evidence. (Initially, the New Jersey State Police wouldn't even allow the agents to see copies of the ransom note.)

The director tried to convince President Herbert Hoover (no relation) to place the FBI in charge of the investigation, but the president refused.

However, on May 12, 1932, when the baby's body was discovered near the Lindbergh home, the president took action. He ordered *all* federal agencies to participate in the investigation. Local authorities were now joined by federal personnel from the Treasury Department's Secret Service Division; the Coast Guard police; the bureaus of Narcotics, Internal Revenue, and Prohibition; the Postal Inspection Service; and the Division of Customs.

Hoover continued to issue press releases that successfully convinced the public that the FBI was in charge. In the minds of most Americans, it was.

Finally, after two and a half years, there was a break in the case. On September 15, 1934, an alert New York City gas station attendant noticed something odd. A driver who had a foreign accent had paid for ninety-eight cents worth of gas with a ten-dollar gold certificate. The driver's accent, the relatively large denomination of the bill, and the fact that it was a gold certificate made the attendant suspicious. (Gold certificates, which are dollar bills redeemable in gold, had been taken out of circulation the year before.) The Treasury Department had requested that gold certificates be included in the ransom money. Lindbergh, not wanting to do anything that would jeopardize getting his son back, disagreed. But the Treasury agents prevailed. When the money was handed over by an intermediary at midnight in a New York cemetery, the telltale bills had been included. Searching Bruno Hauptmann's residence, the police uncovered nearly $15,000 worth of the gold certificates in the garage.

The intermediary who had passed the ransom money that night at the cemetery was asked to identify Hauptmann in a police lineup. The shaken and disheveled Hauptmann was placed next to a dozen clean-shaven and taller men. But the intermediary was unable to make a positive identification.

The Lindbergh ransom money

Lindbergh, who had also gone to the cemetery, did identify Hauptmann. Although he had been unable to see anything in the dark, he testified that it was Hauptmann's voice he had heard that night.

Hauptmann claimed he was innocent. The money had been given to him by someone who had returned to Germany and died, he said. Few believed him.

Bruno Richard Hauptmann (*middle*)

Hauptmann was found guilty and, on April 3, 1936, he was electrocuted.

The trial of Bruno Richard Hauptmann remains one of the most sensational and controversial in American history.

In October, 1991, Anna Hauptmann, his 92-year-old widow, pleaded for a reopening of the case. She has never stopped trying to clear her husband's name. "From the day he was arrested, he was framed, always framed," Mrs. Hauptmann said at a news conference held at the same hotel she had stayed at fifty-six years earlier.

The kidnapping of the Lindbergh baby was a major reason for changes in the law. Congress was reluctant to act as long as there were hopes that the baby was alive. But when the body was discovered they passed what became known as the "Lindbergh Law."

The initial law was passed in June, 1932, and amended two years later. The FBI was given jurisdiction in kidnapping cases where the victim had been taken across state lines. (If the victim had not been returned after seven days, it was assumed this had occurred.) Kidnappers faced the death penalty for what was now a federal crime.

By the time of the kidnapping of Charles Urschel, the "Lindbergh Law" was in effect. The publicity surrounding the Lindbergh case made it the biggest kidnapping the FBI had been involved in. But the case involving the abduction of the Oklahoma oil millionaire was a better example of what was to become classic FBI investigation procedures.

On July 23, 1933, at 11:25 P.M., Charles Urschel and his wife were playing bridge with another couple. Two men, one armed with a machine gun and the other holding a pistol, kidnapped Urschel. Although they warned his wife not to call anyone, she phoned the police as soon as they drove away.

The police directed her to call the FBI, which now had an emergency number to report kidnappings. The call was switched to Hoover's home via his direct line to headquarters. The director immediately ordered agents to the scene of the crime. Four days later, a ransom note arrived demanding $200,000 in cash. The money was paid, and when Urschel was released — unharmed — the FBI moved in on the case.

While being questioned by special agents, Urschel remembered his kidnapping in amazing detail, even though he had been blindfolded. He was able to estimate the size of the car he had been transported in, lying face down on the floor. He remembered crossing a long rattling bridge. When the car stopped for gas, Urschel had heard one of the kidnappers (eager not to act suspicious) make conversation with the gas station attendant. The kidnapper had asked how crop conditions were. The attendant had answered that the corn in the area was almost "burned up" due to lack of rain.

Urschel knew he was being held on a farm because he heard chickens and cows. He could hear the squeak of the pulley as water was drawn from a well, water that had a strong mineral taste. Urschel had done his best to leave fingerprints all over the room he was confined in. Listening carefully, he was able to describe his captors' voices.

Urschel also heard planes passing overhead at 9:45 A.M. and 5:45 P.M. One day there was a rainstorm, and no planes.

FBI agents began patiently putting together the pieces of the puzzle.

The agents checked all airlines that had flights within 600 miles of Urschel's Oklahoma City home. They studied weather reports and isolated an area that was suffering from drought, an area where it was reported that the corn was beginning to burn.

FBI agents scrutinized airline schedules till they found what they were looking for. An airline had a flight from Fort Worth to Amarillo, Texas, that passed over the drought area at the times Urschel had specified. And on one Sunday, the planes had detoured north to avoid a rainstorm. That was all the confirmation they needed.

The FBI suspected "Machine Gun" Kelly might be involved in the Urschel kidnapping. Kelly was born George Baines Kelly and grew up in Memphis. He started out as a bootlegger, but soon turned to burglary and bank robbery. His wife had given him his nickname because she thought it would help build his reputation. Kelly and his wife decided to try their hand at kidnapping. They scanned the society pages of the local papers for wealthy targets. Charles Urschel was to be their last.

FBI agents kept Kelly's mother-in-law's farm, where he was known to hide out, under surveillance. The farm was in Paris, Texas, where the Fort Worth to Amarillo flight passed overhead.

But when agents closed in on the farm, Kelly was gone. It wasn't too long, however, before they caught up with him and arrested him in his Memphis hideout.

"Machine Gun" Kelly (*center*)

A month later, on October 12, 1933, Kelly was found guilty as charged and sentenced to life imprisonment. He died of a heart attack in 1954 while still in prison.

The Urschel case could not have been solved without a coordinated nationwide investigation. Large numbers of agents were called upon to spend countless hours scrutinizing weather reports and comparing them to flight schedules. A variety of evidence had to be analyzed by a modern, scientific crime lab. The Urschel investigation was to become a landmark in FBI history.

The Urschel case became known for another reason. It was where the FBI agents got the nickname G-Men, or so the story goes.

When "Machine Gun" Kelly was finally cornered, he was reported to have cried out, "Don't shoot, G-Men, don't shoot." G-Men stood for government men and the name stuck. G-Men became famous.

G-MEN

Kids wore G-Men pajamas to bed and played with G-Men toy machine guns. There were numerous newspaper stories and magazine articles praising them. There was even a magazine called *G-Men*. (One issue contained "The Famous Cases of J. Edgar Hoover.") Members of the magazine's G-Man club were shown how to take fingerprints with flour and told the secret whistle used by real G-Men (two long, one short). There was also a popular radio program called "The FBI at Peace and War."

G-Men appeared in fifty gangster films in the 1930s, including *Public Hero No. 1*, *Let 'em Have It*, and *Show 'em No Mercy*. *G-Men*, with James Cagney in the lead role, was the most popular of these and it did the most to establish the FBI agent as a hero in the eyes of the American public.

Hoover allowed Hollywood's directors and producers to use FBI files to find plots. He believed that the movies could help him combat the glamourous image of the gangsters. Criminals (whom Hoover referred to as "scum," "rats," "vermin," and "vultures") would not, he vowed, "get away with it." Not in the face of the modern, scientific crime-fighting methods of the FBI. Those who disobeyed the law — especially federal law — would be tracked down, no matter what it took.

The filming of *You Can't Get Away With It*, one of the many movies glorifying the
G-Men

As the FBI's reputation grew, so did Hoover's. Photographers followed him to boxing matches and nightclubs. Whatever he said was newsworthy, especially if it had to do with law and order.

Hoover was so popular there were even rumors he would run for president.

The FBI's reputation as the nation's most effective force against criminals can be traced to the 1930s. At the time, the FBI was perceived as combating a national crime wave. But the crime wave did not exist.

Crime statistics of the time indicate that the amount of criminal activity was actually declining.

A number of factors went into creating the idea of a national crime wave. One was the spectacular and violent nature of the crimes that *were* occurring: daring bank robberies, kidnappings that outraged the nation, and gang wars that led to shoot-outs in the streets.

Reporters eager to sell newspapers, and radio stars hoping to attract listeners, gave a great deal of publicity to a handful of celebrity gangsters.

Only one more element had been needed to convince the American public that there was indeed a national crime wave. And that element was J. Edgar Hoover.

Hoover was appalled by the public's perception of hoodlums like "Ma" Barker, "Old Creepy" Karpis, "Pretty Boy" Floyd, "Machine Gun" Kelly, and John Dillinger as heroes. He believed that a symbol of law and order was needed to counter their glamorous image. He decided that he and his G-Men would become that symbol. He and the FBI would come to stand as incorruptible fighters in a crusade against crime: "We must not for a moment lose sight of our goal, to teach the criminal that, regardless of his subterfuges, his squirming, his twisting and slimy wriggling, he cannot escape the one inexorable rule of law enforcement — 'You can't get away with it.' "

To create this positive image, Hoover saw to it that the FBI's successes were exaggerated and its failures played down. The role of local law enforcement agencies in tracking down criminals was minimalized. Most of the nation's press eagerly went along with Hoover's slanted publicity releases. In the end it was always the FBI that made the final arrest or the spectacular capture — dead or alive.

Hoover almost exclusively concentrated the FBI's resources on the criminals who terrorized the Midwest in the early and mid-1930s. But while he did this, other serious crimes were allowed to flourish without federal intervention.

Hoover refused to recognize the early rise of criminal organizations that were beginning to dominate crime in the big cities: Boston, New York, Chicago, Philadelphia, Detroit, and Los Angeles. Cartels that were to become known in the next two decades as the Mafia.

The Mafia's operation in the United States can be traced back as far as the late 1880s. Members were known to have had meetings in the U.S. in 1928 (New York State), 1929 (Atlantic City — where Al Capone was in attendance), and 1931 (Cleveland). The Federal Bureau of Narcotics, big-city police, and a number of newspaper writers recognized the dangerous growth of organized crime. But in 1933, Hoover stated flatly that a national crime conspiracy did not exist. He took this position for a number of reasons.

Hoover had become obsessed with maintaining the FBI's reputation for achieving a high conviction rate. High conviction rates led to bigger budgets, and bigger budgets led to more power, something else that Hoover had become obsessed with. Cases involving members of organized crime were difficult and complicated to prosecute. Convictions in bank robberies and kidnappings were easier to obtain. The high-priced lawyers maintained by major mob figures were able to mount sophisticated defenses that all too often resulted in hung juries or acquittals.

Al Capone

Newspapers were more likely to cover a blazing shoot-out than they were a lengthy trial. And newspaper coverage was essential to the image Hoover was trying to establish. But it was precisely these kinds of legal proceedings that were needed to break the hold that these urban criminals were beginning to have on American cities.

Another factor was the lack of informants. Many FBI investigations were aided by a critical tip from someone who had spotted a criminal's car or hideout. Other criminals often fingered their cohorts to avoid prosecution for their own crimes (as in the case of John Dillinger). But cracking the code of silence that surrounded the secret society of the Mafia was difficult at best.

Hoover also feared that FBI agents would become corrupted if the bureau took on organized crime. There had been no corruption scandals in the bureau since Hoover had taken over ten years earlier. Hoover was

Bloody gunfights were all too frequent during the Depression, as in the 1935 shooting of Dutch Schultz.

proud of this record. He was reluctant to expose his agents to the kind of money and threats that might be offered by the Mafia. He was concerned that undercover FBI agents planted in long-term assignments within Mafia families would no longer be under his strict control.

For thirty years, Hoover maintained his position that there was no organized crime in America. Since there was no national crime syndicate, it remained a local, not a federal, problem. His position was wrong. It is difficult to believe that the director of the Federal Bureau of Investigation was truly unaware of the existence of the Mafia. His inability to confront the Mafia in these early years is one of his greatest failures.

While J. Edgar Hoover stubbornly stuck to his position, men like Charles "Lucky" Luciano, Frank Costello, Albert Anastasia, "Bugsy" Siegel, Meyer Lansky, and Vito Genovese spread gambling, racketeering (such as taking money from legitimate businesses by force or threat of violence), and drug trafficking throughout the United States.

Meyer Lansky

CHAPTER FIVE

★

THE FBI GOES TO WAR

"Between 1938 and 1945, FBI investigations resulted in ninety-one spying convictions, most of the arrests coming in the first few months after Pearl Harbor. By any measure, German and Japanese undercover operations were a miserable failure. By that standard, the FBI's performance was a brilliant success."

Author Richard Gid Powers

At 7:55 A.M., Sunday, December 7, 1941, the U.S. Pacific Fleet anchored at Pearl Harbor, Hawaii, was attacked by 360 Japanese divebombers and torpedo planes. The operation came as a surprise to the U.S. Navy and the losses were extensive. Fourteen ships were lost, 170 planes destroyed on the ground, and over two thousand Americans killed. Back on the mainland, radio programs were interrupted as Americans were informed of the shocking news.

J. Edgar Hoover was spending a cold Sunday afternoon with thousands of other fans watching a football game between the Washington Redskins and the Philadelphia Eagles. He was asked to leave his box to take an important call. He could hear enemy planes droning in the background as the FBI agent in charge of the Honolulu office informed him: "The Japanese are bombing Pearl Harbor. . . . It's war."

The next day, Monday, December 8, 1941, the Congress of the United States declared war on Japan. The United States would now join its British allies who had been fighting for over two years.

Japan attacked Pearl Harbor on December 7, 1941.

President Franklin Roosevelt and Director Hoover were prepared. Both wanted to avoid the confusion and lack of coordination that characterized the government's efforts against spies and saboteurs during World War I. Then, twenty different agencies had divided the responsibility of protecting the home front. Too often, operations by German enemy agents had been successful.

In 1936, even before the United States entered the war, President Roosevelt had authorized Hoover to gather information regarding any potential acts of espionage or sabotage. There were then an estimated one million German, Italian, and Japanese aliens living in the United States. Now that America was at war with these countries, Roosevelt feared that some of them might commit acts of sabotage. He discussed with Hoover steps to prevent this from happening. The president also asked Hoover to keep an eye on suspected enemy agents.

To meet the bureau's new responsibilities, Hoover began to increase the number of FBI employees. In 1924 there had been 441 FBI agents. By 1940 there were 898, and by 1941 that number had nearly doubled. There were almost 5,000 FBI agents in 1944. The total number of FBI employees reached 13,317 by the end of the war.

In 1939, Roosevelt had expanded the FBI's responsibilities. The president had sent a secret memo to Hoover stating:

> You are therefore authorized and directed . . . to authorize the necessary investigating agents that they are at liberty to secure the information by listening devices directed to the conversations or other communications of persons suspected of subversive activity against the Government of the United States, including suspected spies. You are requested furthermore to limit these investigations so conducted to a minimum and to limit them in so far as possible to aliens.

Roosevelt's action is, to this day, considered controversial. Many historians believe that Roosevelt had no legal right to ask Hoover to do this, and that Hoover had no legal right doing it. A decision had been made to spy on Americans who had not committed any crimes. Who was to decide if someone was a suspected spy? How much information was needed to make someone suspect? The mere suspicion that people might be involved in espionage now gave the FBI the power to violate their rights as private citizens. And the decision as to whether or not this was justified was left entirely in the hands of one man — J. Edgar Hoover.

A memo was sent to agents in the field commanding them to "obtain from all possible sources information concerning subversive activities taking place in the United States." Local police were instructed to relay to their nearest FBI office any information about suspicious activities. Citizens were urged to do the same. "Don't investigate anything yourself," was one popular slogan. "Report it to the FBI," was another.

Hoover reported a dramatic increase in the number of spy cases. Between 1933 and 1937, the FBI had investigated an average of 35 espionage cases a year. By the time the war ended, the FBI reported nearly 20,000 cases of suspected espionage.

Hoover had already decided to re-establish the General Intelligence Division. The GID had been abolished under orders from Attorney General Stone in 1924, Hoover's first year as director. Now, for the first time since that year, the FBI would be investigating what people believed and thought, *not* what they actually did. The limitations that Attorney General Stone had imposed on the bureau had been removed by Franklin Roosevelt.

Hoover charged his agents with preventing acts of sabotage, not merely catching the guilty parties. Agents inspected 2,350 key war production plants and made recommendations to tighten security. The FBI provided war-related industries with instructions on preventing fires and making their plants sabotage-proof. An FBI team studied the British civil defense system, and then field agents instructed local authorities on what they had learned.

Throughout the war years, the FBI acted swiftly and efficiently. The years of preparation were paying off. The bureau was well versed in Nazi espionage tactics. One key discovery was the secret of microdots.

The FBI was aware of the many ways secret information could be passed: messages concealed inside what looked like fountain pens, paper dotted with nearly invisible pin pricks, and codes of various kinds. The bureau learned via a double agent that the Nazis had developed a way to reduce a full page of type to the size of a tiny dot, no bigger than the period at the end of a sentence. After enlarging the dot 200 times, the message could be read easily. Knowledge of this advance in technology aided the bureau in its efforts against spies and saboteurs.

One important case involved a German-born American citizen named William Sebold. Sebold had been blackmailed by the Gestapo, the German secret police. If he refused to spy for them, they threatened to harm his relatives, who were still living in Germany. Sebold confided his dilemma to the FBI, who transformed him into a double agent.

Through Sebold, the FBI transmitted a mixture of true and false information to the unaware Gestapo. German agents who delivered stolen information to Sebold's office were secretly photographed by the FBI through a one-way mirror and recorded through a hidden microphone.

The FBI let the German spies continue until they were sure the entire spy ring was known to them. Then, on June 28, 1941, they moved in. Thirty-three spies were arrested and charged with violating espionage statutes. All were found guilty and sentenced to a total of 320 years in prison.

The biggest spy ring ever known to operate within the United States had been destroyed by the FBI.

★　★　★

One of the most publicized cases in FBI history began shortly after midnight on June 13, 1942. Four German saboteurs were seen with a large raft on the beach near Amagansett, Long Island. A Coast Guard seaman making his midnight patrol encountered them and, within twelve hours, the FBI had been notified. J. Edgar Hoover then ordered a nationwide manhunt and placed all FBI field offices on full alert. This resulted in their capture, which was announced by Hoover at a news conference on June 27, 1942. Details of the FBI's seizure of the Germans were to be kept secret until after the war. The headlines told the story: FBI CAPTURES 8 GERMAN AGENTS LANDED BY SUBS.

The true story, however, was much more complicated.

The four German saboteurs had been landed by submarine on the Long Island beach. They were chosen for their mission, in part, because they had once lived in the United States. They had been schooled in the art of industrial sabotage, including how to incapacitate industrial machines, blow up bridges, and cripple railroads. They were supplied with explosives, fuses, and timing mechanisms. Their instructions were to leave no doubt that their actions had been the result of sabotage. Spreading terror in America was a significant part of their objective.

Equally important were the false life histories they had memorized and the fake ID's they carried: birth certificates, Social Security cards, and drivers' licenses. They also had $84,000 in cash.

Up to the time they reached America's shores, the operation went as planned. From that point forward it was, however, a fiasco.

When the Coast Guard seaman encountered them, the Germans were struggling to get their rubber raft ashore. Taken by surprise, they claimed to be fishermen. But the only thing fishy was their story. The seaman heard one speak German and spotted what appeared to be a submarine offshore. His suspicions were confirmed when he was offered a bribe to keep silent.

Unarmed, he accepted the bribe and reported the incident as soon as he returned to his station. His superiors initially doubted his report. Had they not hesitated, the four saboteurs would probably have been apprehended before they left the beach. When they did investigate, at dawn, they found explosives contained in waterproof boxes and the German uniforms that had been left there.

The FBI was notified by the local police and the field offices were ordered on full alert.

Meanwhile, a strange scenario was unfolding.

George John Dasch, the German operations leader, had lived in the United States for twenty years. His motives for what occurred next are the subject of much debate. One interpretation is that he was, from the outset, more sympathetic to the United States than to Germany. A second factor is that he was frightened that he would be caught and executed because of the seaman's chance discovery. In all probability, both factors played a role in Dasch's decision to turn himself in to the FBI.

Dasch called the FBI's New York office, where it was considered a crank call — it wasn't even logged in! Dasch then decided to surrender directly to J. Edgar Hoover. He took the train to Washington, where he again had difficulty convincing the FBI that he wasn't a nut. Finally, however, Hoover was contacted.

The FBI interrogated Dasch for eight days. He gave them valuable information about his mission as well as the German war effort in general. He told the FBI where they could pick up the other three members of his crew and of a second team that was to land off the coast of Florida.

Within days, all eight saboteurs of the two ill-fated teams had been arrested.

Dasch's surrender was not made public at the time. As a wartime procedure this was not unusual: the less the Germans knew about the capture, the better. But what was curious was Hoover's decision not to inform President Roosevelt. Hoover gave a different date for Dasch's capture to the president. By making it seem that Dasch had been caught with the others, he could keep the true story of how the FBI cracked the case from Roosevelt and the public. Thus he could insure the continued glorification of the Federal Bureau of Investigation.

The FBI's capture of the eight German saboteurs was a major step in the bureau's becoming America's foremost federal agency; an all-knowing, invincible shield against the country's enemies.

All eight were tried, convicted, and sentenced to death. Six of them were executed. Dasch and a member of his crew who had also cooperated with the FBI were pardoned in 1948 by President Harry S. Truman. They were deported to Germany, where they were considered traitors.

The FBI reported that of the nearly 20,000 cases of suspected espionage or sabotage that were investigated, not one was successful. Although Hoover continued the image-polishing he had begun in the 1930s, there is no denying the excellent performance of the bureau during World War II. It played an important role in preventing Nazi spies and saboteurs from doing any damage.

By August, 1945, when the United States dropped the atomic bomb on the Japanese cities of Hiroshima and Nagasaki, the war was over. The United States and her allies, England and the Soviet Union, had emerged victorious.

The use of the atomic bomb effectively ended World War II.

CHAPTER SIX

★

THE COLD WAR YEARS

"McCarthy is America's most controversial figure. J. Edgar Hoover is its most feared."

Journalist I. F. Stone

"Un-American is simply something that somebody else does not agree to."

Congressman Maury Maverick

After World War II, the United States and the Soviet Union were the dominant powers in the world. The Russian people had fought heroically against the Germans, winning the admiration of their American allies. The Soviet Union had played a critical role in the defeat of Hitler's Germany.

The good feeling did not last long, however. Mutual distrust by the two country's leaders created a hostile, postwar period.

This period became known as the Cold War era. It began soon after the war ended and continued until 1991 and the breakup of the Soviet Union. The term was most often used, however, in the 1950s and early 1960s. These were the years when there was no actual shooting war (or hot war) between the U.S. and the U.S.S.R., but there was a constant atmosphere of hostility and tension. Both countries took political, economic, and military steps that created a fear that actual military conflict — World War III — might erupt.

The Soviet Union was considered a dangerous threat now that the war against the Nazis had been won. Many people believed that the communists in America were being secretly directed by the Russian government. Their goal was thought to be nothing less than the takeover of the United States.

Since the Communist Revolution of 1917, some Americans had come to believe in the principles of the communist philosophy of society. As far as they were concerned, communism was a better way of life than capitalism. To these Americans, the Soviet Union was not the enemy of the United States. Some did what they could to help the communists, even if that involved spying on the country of their birth.

The threat of spying by Americans who sympathized with the communists was a real one. However, in the late 1940s and in the 1950s, there were charges that communist sympathizers and spies were around every corner. Attorney General J. Howard McGrath warned: "There are today many Communists in America. They are everywhere — in factories, offices, butcher stores, on street corners, in private business."

Journalists, congressmen, celebrities, and businessmen accused co-workers, neighbors, and strangers of being spies, often without proof and often mistakenly. People were publicly accused of being communists because of organizations they belonged to or people they associated with. Belonging to an organization that was considered communist was enough to brand you as a traitor. Suspicion was enough to ruin someone's career. Fear poisoned the atmosphere, and proof was often unnecessary.

In March, 1947, President Harry S. Truman's Executive Order 9835 initiated the Federal Employees Loyalty and Security Program. It applied to all two million federal workers. Anyone who was believed disloyal could no longer work for the federal government, although the term "disloyal" was never defined. Any employee could be dismissed, and any applicant turned down if there were "reasonable grounds for belief that a person is disloyal."

"Reasonable grounds" usually meant that the person was suspected of belonging to a communist organization that sought "to alter the government of the United States by unconstitutional means." The attorney general, with Hoover's help, developed a list of organizations the Justice Department had identified as "disloyal."

The Truman Loyalty Program caused FBI operations to expand. The FBI ran "name checks" on current government employees. If an employee's file came back with the words NO DISLOYAL DATA FBI FILES, the subject of the investigation was considered cleared by the FBI. If there was suspicious information in a person's background check, the FBI passed this information on to a Loyalty Review Board.

If requested, the FBI would make a full investigation. The bureau investigated 14,000 people as a result of the Truman Loyalty Program. Only 212 were dismissed because their loyalty was in question. No one was ever indicted for spying, nor was there any evidence of espionage as a result of these investigations.

But J. Edgar Hoover believed that Executive Order 9835 was not strong enough. He had done everything in his power to convince the president, Congress, and the public that the communist menace he had warned them about in the 1920s was an even greater threat in the 1950s. "The Communist Party-USA is under the complete control and domination of the Soviet Union and as such poses a menace to the security of the country."

He described communism as a disease that could only be prevented by constantly being on guard; a service his FBI would provide. FBI agents were told by Hoover to maintain constant surveillance of communist activities in the United States. Wiretaps were placed when the director considered the nation's security at stake. Anyone who agreed with the communists on any issue was liable to be the subject of an FBI investigation.

Hoover's critics claimed that he was exaggerating the threat. They cited the small number of communists in the United States. But Hoover had a ready reply. "It took only twenty-three men to overthrow Russia." For Hoover the lesson was clear: It *could* happen here.

Two congressional committees were in the forefront of the attack on what they perceived to be widespread subversion within the government and other sectors of American society.

Many Americans felt that these committee hearings were necessary to safeguard U.S. citizens from the threat of being taken over by communists. But many, equally loyal Americans, felt the hearings were more un-American than the activities they were investigating. They were concerned about possible violations of the liberties supposedly guaranteed by the Bill of Rights.

The Bill of Rights, the first ten amendments to the Constitution, was adopted in 1791. In approximately four hundred words they describe the fundamental liberties guaranteed to each individual United States citizen — rights that were not to be violated by the federal government.

Among other things, the Bill of Rights guarantees freedom of speech. Many people believed that the congressional hearings violated that freedom. The Bill of Rights also guarantees "the right to a speedy and public trial" and the right of a citizen "to be confronted with the witnesses against him." Although the hearing chambers were not official courts of law, the people called before the committees seemed to be on trial while being denied their fundamental rights.

THE HOUSE COMMITTEE ON UN-AMERICAN ACTIVITIES

The House Committee on Un-American Activities (HUAC) was established in 1938. It was charged with investigating fascists and communists at a time when both were considered threats to the American way of life. The greater portion of the committee's time was spent investigating alleged communist activities.

Nine years later, in 1947, HUAC continued to play an active role in investigating people and organizations suspected of communist affiliations or outright spying. (It had been made a permanent committee of the House of Representatives two years earlier.)

HUAC's hearings on subversive activities in Hollywood were highly publicized events. The committee believed that communists were attempting to control the movie industry. The 1947 hearings featured the movie stars and movie moguls of the day testifying in front of floodlights, microphones, and television cameras (at a time when television was new). The actors and actresses who provided the names of co-workers they thought might be communists kept the hearings constantly in the headlines.

Movie executives bowed to the patriotic pressures of the day by announcing that they would discharge anyone who didn't cooperate with the committee. A blacklist was developed with the names of known and suspected communists. These people were not hired by the studios. "Red Channels," a booklet of those in the entertainment industry who were blacklisted, was published and followed carefully by show-business executives.

But HUAC had its critics. They charged that the committee's accusations were not supported by evidence. To some, the hearings were a shameful chapter in American history.

One prominent member of the committee was Richard Nixon, a young, California congressman who was destined to become the 37th President of the United States. Nixon later recalled that:

> . . . the Committee in 1948 was under constant and severe attack from many segments of both the press and the public. It had been widely con-

HUAC made or ruined many careers. (*top*) Representative Milton Dies (*right*) confronts the columnist Heywood Broun. (*bottom*) Representative Richard Nixon (*far left*) reads committee transcripts.

demned as a "Red-baiting" group, habitually unfair and irresponsible, whose investigations had failed to lead to a single conviction of anyone against whom charges had been made at its hearings. It was, critics said, doing more of a disservice to the country because of its abridgment of civil liberties than any alleged services it might be rendering in uncovering Communist subversives.

HUAC needed a case that would show that its tactics were justified. They needed something that would convince the public and the press that communists were indeed infiltrating the government and taking over other areas of American life. In the summer of 1948, HUAC got the case it needed.

THE HISS–CHAMBERS CASE

Alger Hiss was a highly respected former State Department official. A Harvard Law School graduate, Hiss had participated in the conference that led to the establishment of the United Nations. He had been a clerk for former Associate Justice of the United States Supreme Court, Oliver Wendell Holmes, Jr., and was affiliated with other prominent Americans.

Hiss was accused of being a communist by Whittaker Chambers. Chambers, an admitted former communist, was a senior editor at *Time* when he appeared before the House Committee on Un-American Activities in the summer of 1948. He testified that in the mid-1930s, Hiss had agreed to provide State Department documents to help the Soviet Union in its fight against fascism during World War II. Chambers named Hiss as one of four members of an underground communist cell, a small secret group.

This stunning accusation became headline news the next day. Hiss was the highest ranking government official to be accused of being a communist spy.

Hiss sent the committee a telegram requesting an opportunity to appear in public session to deny the charge. In early August, Hiss appeared before the committee and stated: "I am not and never have been a member of the Communist Party. I do not and never have adhered to the tenets of the Communist Party. . . . I have never followed the Communist Party line directly or indirectly." He said he did not even know Whittaker Chambers.

On August 17, 1948, Hiss and Chambers met face-to-face. Hiss admitted to the committee that he might have known Chambers under another name. But he continued to deny that he was a communist. A few days later the two met again in a public confrontation that was the first major congressional hearing to be televised. The hearing lasted nine hours. Chambers recounted, in detail, all he knew about Hiss. He told about Hiss's cocker spaniel; Mrs. Hiss's pet name for her husband (Hilly); the inside and outside of the houses the Hisses lived in; Hiss's

Whittaker Chambers (*right*) accusing Alger Hiss of being a communist

hobbies, including specifics about birdwatching, his favorite; and other personal details.

Hiss challenged Chambers to make his accusations outside of the hearing room so that he could sue him for making statements that were false and damaging to his reputation. A few days later, Chambers repeated the charges on television and Hiss filed a $75,000 libel suit.

The high point of the trial was the late-breaking revelation by Chambers that he had microfilm in his possession of State Department documents.

In late December, 1948, at 10:30 P.M., Chambers led two committee investigators to a pumpkin patch on his Maryland farm. Chambers revealed the five rolls of microfilm, hidden inside a hollowed-out pumpkin. The discovery of the "Pumpkin Papers" made the following morning's headlines. Two strips of the microfilm were shown to contain the documents (some in code) that Chambers claimed had been typed by Hiss's wife. This led to one of the most important questions of the case: Were these documents in fact typed on the Hisses' typewriter?

Their typewriter had been given away years ago. Hiss and his attorneys and the FBI launched a nationwide search for it. It was finally located by Hiss's lawyer. But the typewriter pointed to Hiss's guilt, not innocence.

Ramos C. Feehand had been a bureau documents examiner for eleven years. He appeared in court standing on a platform, holding a pointer to show the jury what he saw on the two photo enlargements displayed behind him. Feehand was comparing the documents with letters known to have been typed by Mrs. Hiss. He used the enlargements to illustrate the similarity of certain defects in the keys. According to Feehand, the documents had been typed on the same typewriter, the typewriter once owned by Alger Hiss.

In January, 1950, Hiss was convicted of perjury for having, according to the jury, lied about giving the State Department documents to Chambers. (The statute of limitations on espionage committed in the 1930s had run out, so Hiss could only be charged with having lied in court.) He was given a five-year sentence, and was released from prison in 1954, after being given time off for good behavior.

THE McCARTHY COMMITTEE

The Hiss–Chambers hearings and Hiss's subsequent conviction had a profound influence on the course of modern American history. For one thing, the controversial proceedings propelled committee member Richard Nixon into the national spotlight. The guilty verdict also gave credibility to the anti-communist crusade of Senator Joseph McCarthy.

McCarthy gained national attention in February, 1950, just days after Hiss was found guilty. Addressing a Republican women's club, McCarthy said: "While I cannot take the time to name all the men in the State Department who have been named as members of the Communist party and members of a spy ring, I have here in my hand a list of 205 — a list of names that were made known to the Secretary of State as being members of the Communist party and who nevertheless are still working and shaping policy in the State Department."

McCarthy was never able to find the time to hand over the list of the 205 (the number changed within days of his speech). But his charge of treachery in government was the beginning of an ongoing national news story.

In 1953, McCarthy was appointed Chairman of the Senate Committee on Government Operations. He promptly appointed himself chairman of its powerful subcommittee. The McCarthy Committee, as it came to be called, attacked the State Department, United Nations, Government Printing Office, Voice of America, U.S. Army, and other federal agencies as being under the influence of subversives.

Senator Joseph McCarthy (*left*) and Roy Cohn displaying a letter from J. Edgar Hoover concerning a possible spy

Senator McCarthy appealed to many Americans who believed his unsupported charges that the State Department was filled with spies. He was perceived by them as being fearless in the face of the communist menace. While others, including (according to McCarthy) President Truman, were "soft on communism," McCarthy was not: "Let me assure you that regardless of how high-pitched becomes the squeaking and screaming of left-wing, bleeding heart, phony liberals, this battle is going to go on."

McCarthy considered liberal Americans to be communist sympathizers and worse. He defined patriotism as being anti-communist, and attacked people who weren't. His anti-communist investigations made him one of the most controversial figures in American politics. The nation's newspapers, with rare exception, eagerly awaited the senator's next sensational accusation and invariably gave him page-one billing. McCarthy made good copy, and good copy sold newspapers.

When his accusations were shown to be untrue, which they usually were, he simply came up with new ones. His style was crude and he was not above hitting below the belt by using half-truths and outright lies. More often than not, his information was untrue and his accusations false. At press conferences and committee hearings, McCarthy spoke of a briefcase full of incriminating documents obtained by methods he could not divulge. His style of politics came to be called McCarthyism, defined as "the practice of making accusations of disloyalty, especially of pro-communist activities, often unsupported or based on doubtful evidence."

Senator McCarthy testifying during the Army–McCarthy hearings

His downfall came in the spring of 1954, when he attacked the U.S. Army. McCarthy claimed that there were subversives in the army. McCarthy further charged that the army command, as high up as the Pentagon, had tried to block his investigation in order to protect themselves.

The nationally televised Army–McCarthy hearings were among the most dramatic confrontations in American political history. The Army's able and eloquent lawyer, Joseph Welch, showed McCarthy for what he was: a crude bully who attacked innocent people without just cause. McCarthy did not come off as well on camera as he did in print.

In December, 1954, the Senate voted to condemn him for actions unbecoming a senator. He died three years later of acute hepatitis, though the press hinted (correctly) that he drank himself to death.

HOOVER, HUAC, AND McCARTHY

The House Committee on Un-American Activities (HUAC) and the McCarthy Committee would not have been able to function without the constant cooperation of J. Edgar Hoover and the FBI.

HUAC pursued a course that Hoover had pioneered thirty years before. Ten years earlier, in 1939, Hoover created the Custodial Detention list, which said that "both aliens and citizens of the United States, on whom there is information available that their presence at liberty in this country in time of war or national emergency would be dangerous to the public peace and safety of the United States Government" would be detained. (The Custodial Detention list was later named the less-ominous-sounding Security Index.) The Custodial Detention program continued into the 1950s. Hoover compiled a list of all individuals in the United States who would be, in his opinion, dangerous in the event of war with the Soviet Union.

Hoover saw to it that the FBI worked closely with the two congressional committees. He ordered FBI agents to make bureau files available to committee members. (Hoover did not allow the actual "raw" files to be read by the committee. The files were changed into "reports" and it was these reports that were given to the committees.) Undercover FBI agents appeared as key witnesses at the hearings.

The hearings gave Hoover a much desired public forum for exposing the information the FBI had gathered. Information obtained by the bureau via informants, telephone wiretaps, hidden microphones, and other surveillance methods, was readily supplied, behind the scenes, to favored committee members.

Hoover's aides provided HUAC with lists of Hollywood artists who were believed to be members of communist organizations. They produced another list of anti-communists in the Hollywood community who might supply the names of people they considered disloyal Americans. These people were called "friendly witnesses."

Senator McCarthy (*left*) and Robert Kennedy (*right*) at the HUAC hearings

The name of one "friendly witness" provided by Hoover was Ronald Reagan, then president of the Screen Actors Guild. Reagan acted as a "confidential informant," naming actors and actresses who were considered subversive. With Reagan's help, HUAC was able to have these people blacklisted and, in most cases, to end their careers.

Hoover also worked closely with McCarthy. They had been friends as well as political allies since 1946: "I never knew Senator McCarthy until he came to the Senate. I've come to know him well, officially and personally. I view him as a friend and believe he so views me. Certainly he is a controversial man. He is earnest and he is honest. He has enemies. Whenever you attack subversives . . . you are going to be the victim of the most extremely vicious criticism that can be made."

In 1948, Hoover invited McCarthy to address the graduating class of the FBI's National Academy. By 1953, a number of former FBI agents were working on McCarthy's staff, including his chief investigator. After a while, McCarthy's office became known as "the little FBI."

The FBI's scope of activities expanded greatly in the 1950s as a result of the Truman Loyalty Program and the ongoing congressional hunt for communists and subversives.

But the decade's most controversial trial was taking place against this backdrop of anti-communist passions. It was the trial of two Americans who Hoover said had committed "the crime of the century."

THE ROSENBERGS

In early February, 1950, a month after Alger Hiss was convicted, Klaus Fuchs was arrested in England. Fuchs had become a British citizen after fleeing Nazi Germany in 1937. A brilliant physicist and mathematician, he had been involved in the greatest scientific project in history: the race to create an atomic bomb.

During World War II, the United States government had feared that German nuclear physicists were developing an atomic bomb. In the spring of 1943, the United States began a program that was so secret most government, military, and congressional leaders were not advised of its existence. Even Harry Truman, when he was vice-president (soon to be president), had not been told.

A team of distinguished scientists, led by J. Robert Oppenheimer, was assembled in Los Alamos, a small town in New Mexico. Isolated from the outside world, they worked to design and construct the first atomic bomb. The top secret, two-billion-dollar project was a success. An atomic bomb was dropped on the Japanese city of Hiroshima on August 6, 1945. Three days later another, more powerful bomb was dropped on Nagasaki. The light from the explosion was three times brighter than the midday sun. The most destructive weapon yet developed had been unleashed.

In September, 1949, President Truman announced that the Soviet Union had exploded its first atomic bomb. The awesome power of the atomic bomb no longer belonged exclusively to the United States.

During the war, many scientists had felt that the Soviet Union, then America's ally, should be informed about the bomb. At the time it was a controversial issue. Some scientists felt that the Russians would be capable of making an atomic bomb within five years, even without America's help.

Now, however, many Americans believed that the Russians had stolen the secrets of the atomic bomb. BRITISH JAIL ATOM SCIENTIST AS A SPY AFTER TIP BY F.B.I. read a headline in *The New York Times*. One of those who was convinced that espionage was involved was FBI Director Hoover. He immediately mobilized the resources of the Federal Bureau of Investigation. "The secret of the atomic bomb has been stolen. Find the thieves," he ordered.

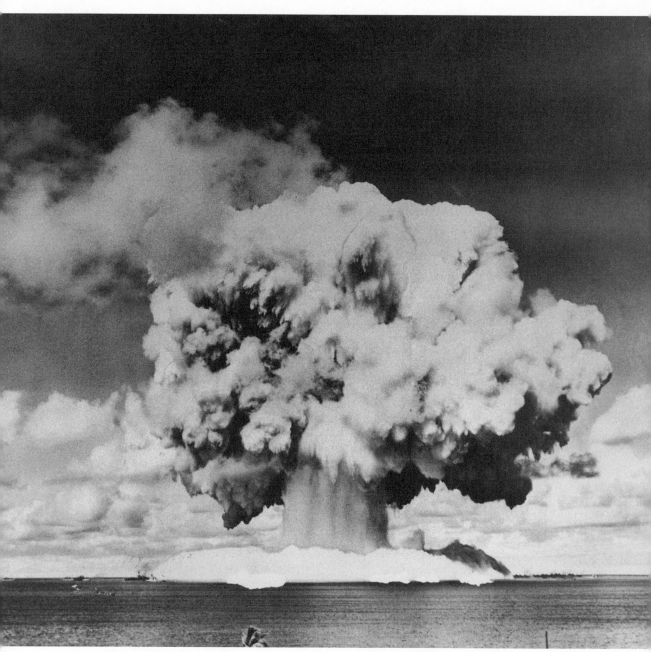

The atomic bomb was the most powerful weapon ever unleashed.

FBI agents interviewed hundreds of people and searched the files at Los Alamos and other sites where research had been done. A few months later, Klaus Fuchs was arrested. The FBI, working with British intelligence, had identified Fuchs as a Russian spy.

Fuchs had worked in Los Alamos for three years. He admitted passing top secret information to agents of the Soviet Union. His trial lasted only one hour and twenty-seven minutes. Fuchs was sentenced to fourteen years in prison — the maximum allowable under British law.

The FBI discovered that Fuchs had an American accomplice known to him only by the code name "Raymond." Fuchs gave the FBI a vague description of "Raymond": around forty years old, approximately five feet ten inches tall, with a broad build and a round face.

Less than three months later, in May, 1950, Hoover announced the arrest of Harry Gold, a Philadelphia chemist. "In all the history of the FBI," Hoover declared, "there never was a more important problem than this one, never another case where we felt under such pressure . . . the unknown man simply had to be found."

FBI agents began questioning Harry Gold, who confessed that he was "Raymond," Fuchs's American contact. Gold's confession led the FBI to David Greenglass. Greenglass was a young soldier who had been stationed in Los Alamos during the war. He, too, was arrested and confessed that he had given information on the atomic bomb to Harry Gold.

Greenglass told the FBI that his brother-in-law and sister, Julius and Ethel Rosenberg, had convinced him to become a spy. The Rosenbergs, according to Greenglass, argued that the Russians were America's allies, fighting the same enemy. It was wrong not to share information with them. Greenglass admitted that he gave the Rosenbergs secret information from Los Alamos.

In early July, 1950, David Greenglass was indicted on a charge of

Klaus Fuchs (*left*) and Ethel and
Julius Rosenberg (*below*) were all
convicted of giving the secrets of
the atomic bomb to the Russians.

conspiring to commit espionage in wartime. Days later, FBI agents arrested his brother-in-law, Julius Rosenberg, and a month later, agents arrested Rosenberg's wife, Ethel, both on the same charge.

Julius and Ethel Rosenberg were native New Yorkers with two small sons, seven and three. Julius was an electrical engineer who had been involved in radical politics for many years. After the war, Julius Rosenberg and David Greenglass had owned a small machine shop in New York City. Hoover described Julius Rosenberg as "another important link in the Soviet espionage apparatus which included Dr. Klaus Fuchs."

The Rosenberg trial began in New York City on March 6, 1951. The courtroom was crowded. Most people had come to see the "atom spies" convicted. But there were also those who felt the Rosenbergs were innocent. The atmosphere was tense and there was an eerie silence as the trial opened.

David Greenglass testified against the Rosenbergs. Greenglass told the court that Julius Rosenberg had convinced him to turn over secret information. He said he gave Julius Rosenberg handwritten notes which Julius had Ethel Rosenberg type. This information included scientific data, sketches, and a list of scientists for possible recruitment.

Greenglass told about one evening when Julius Rosenberg took a Jell-O box from the kitchen cabinet. He removed the contents and cut one of the sides of the box into two oddly shaped pieces. He kept one piece and told David that the other half would be given to a contact man. Once given the matching piece of the Jell-O box, Greenglass was to hand the information over to that man. When this mysterious future meeting came about, the other half of the Jell-O box appeared in the hands of confessed spy Harry Gold, Klaus Fuchs's American contact. The Gold–Greenglass meeting had been uncovered by FBI agents during their questioning of Greenglass. This testimony tied Greenglass and Rosenberg to Gold, who had already confessed his relationship with Fuchs.

Greenglass said that when Fuchs was arrested, Julius Rosenberg warned him to leave the country. Greenglass claimed that Rosenberg controlled a network of spies working in the United States. And that this network included Greenglass's sister, Ethel.

The government alleged that the Rosenbergs had criminally conspired with Greenglass and his wife, Ruth, Harry Gold, and others to provide the Soviet Union with the secret of the atomic bomb. Federal prosecutors claimed that Julius and Ethel Rosenberg were spies and should be punished for their crimes.

The Rosenbergs denied all charges against them.

They claimed that David Greenglass was providing the FBI with false information about Julius Rosenberg being a master spy because he hoped to receive a lesser sentence for himself. The Rosenbergs claimed his story was pure fiction.

They also said that Greenglass held a grudge against them because of the failure of the machine shop they had jointly owned and was allowing a family feud to assume horrible proportions.

"History will record," Julius Rosenberg said, "whether we live or not, that we were the victims of the most monstrous frame-up in the history of the country."

The Rosenbergs and their supporters believed that they were being persecuted because of the current anti-communist atmosphere in America. That atmosphere had worsened the year before, in June, 1950, when troops from communist North Korea, helped by Chinese troops and Soviet supplies, invaded South Korea. U.S. air, naval, and ground forces had been sent to aid the South Koreans. The Korean War (1950–1953) continued to be fought during the Rosenberg trial.

The FBI, the Rosenbergs believed, was pressuring them into naming others, higher up the ladder. They felt that Ethel Rosenberg had been arrested in order to force her husband to confess to a crime he never committed. They were being used by the government as a warning to other would-be spies.

The Rosenbergs pointed out that the government's case against them was insufficient. The FBI had not found any evidence of espionage. There were no shortwave radios, microfilm equipment, miniature cameras, stolen documents, code books, or forged passports.

Greenglass and Gold might be spies but they — Julius and Ethel Rosenberg — knew nothing of their activities. The Rosenbergs maintained their innocence throughout the trial.

On March 29, 1951, the jury found them guilty of conspiring to commit espionage. Five days later, on April 5, the judge sentenced them both to die in the electric chair: "I consider your crime worse than murder. Plain deliberate contemplated murder is dwarfed in magnitude by comparison with the crime you have committed. . . . Indeed, by your betrayal, you undoubtedly have altered the course of history to the disadvantage of our country."

The trial had been sensational and controversial. The verdict and the judge's sentence were even more controversial. To some, the Rosenbergs were spies who had given the secrets of the world's most powerful weapon to America's communist enemy. They were criminals who were caught and who got what was coming to them. To others, they were victims who suffered from the paranoia in America that saw communists, spies, and traitors everywhere.

For two years, the Rosenbergs waited on death row. Their case was reviewed sixteen times by the United States District Court. Seven appeals were denied by the United States Supreme Court.

Twice, President Eisenhower was asked to grant them clemency, and twice he refused.

On the evening of June 19, 1953, the Rosenbergs died in the electric chair in New York's Sing Sing prison. They became the first American

The execution of the Rosenbergs caused deep division around the country.

citizens to be put to death for wartime spying. It was also the first execution of a husband and wife, and the first execution of a woman by the United States government in ninety years.

David Greenglass was sentenced to fifteen years for his crimes. He was released in 1960 and currently lives, with his wife, in New York City.

For J. Edgar Hoover and the Federal Bureau of Investigation, the case was a major success. At the trial, the judge thanked Hoover for the excellent job done by the bureau.

PART TWO

---★---

THE YEARS OF CONTROVERSY

"... the most successful job of salesmanship
in the history of western bureaucracy."
                                    Writer Robert Sherrill

"If some of those people stop criticizing me,
I'd be worried that somehow I wasn't doing
my job right."
                                    J. Edgar Hoover

CHAPTER SEVEN

★

"THE BOSS"

"Tolson [Associate Director of the FBI] would say, 'This is what the Boss wants. If the Boss wants that, that's what he's going to get. The Boss thinks we ought to do it this way and that's the way we're going to do it. Now fix it up, get a memo so it reads that way. I'll tell the Boss.' "

Former Assistant Director
of the Crime Records Division, Robert Wick

J. Edgar Hoover had worked tirelessly to build the Federal Bureau of Investigation into one of the most respected branches of the United States government. Hoover was a perfectionist and his dedication to the bureau was total: The FBI was his life.

When he took over the bureau, many (maybe most) agents were incompetent or corrupt (sometimes both); standards had been slack; guidelines non-existent.

Twenty-five years later Hoover could proudly refer to his agents as "the most carefully selected men in the world." They were considered the standard for all other law enforcement agencies. FBI agents were supposed to be clean-living family men; churchgoing and upstanding members of their communities; honest men dedicated to the fight against crime. No agent in Hoover's long reign as director had ever been charged with a crime committed while on duty. J. Edgar Hoover's FBI agents protected law-abiding citizens from political radicals, robbers, traitors, killers, and kidnappers. They were to stand guard, defending the American way of life.

An FBI employee knew he might be fired for even the slightest violation of the rules, written or unwritten. Hair was to be kept short, suits well-pressed, and shirts white. Even not paying your personal bills on time could bring a bureau reprimand.

J. Edgar Hoover proudly accepted his role symbolizing the FBI. Indeed, it was a role he invited: "As long as I am Director of this Bureau any attack on an FBI employee who is conscientiously carrying out his official duties will be considered an attack on me personally."

Hoover was viewed by most Americans as an awesome figure — someone to be feared, but respected. Confident, with a no-nonsense manner, he was relentless in his pursuit of those he considered criminals.

Hoover's achievements in the field of scientific criminal investigation have earned him a worldwide reputation. And they have been lasting achievements: a vast computerized universe of retrievable information on crime and criminals available to law enforcement agencies around the country; the services of a state-of-the-art FBI lab; and the founding of the National Academy police training facilities which allow modern crime-fighting techniques to be made available to police forces throughout the United States. No one contributed more to modern law-enforcement techniques than J. Edgar Hoover.

In 1958, Hoover added to his prestige when his *Masters of Deceit* became a bestseller. It sold 250,000 copies in hardcover and two million in paperback.

The overwhelming majority of Americans considered J. Edgar Hoover a public servant who could do no wrong. But there were those who disagreed. They felt that the public's perception had been manipulated by Hoover.

Walter Trohan, Washington bureau chief for *The Chicago Tribune*, was an early doubter of Hoover's flawless reputation: "For subtle mixture of fact and fancy the career of J. Edgar Hoover, No. 1 G-Man . . . is a fascinating study in the molding of a myth."

Newspaper columnist Westbrook Pegler, another early Hoover critic, wrote in 1938:

> Do you want to know something about Mr. Hoover? He is spoiled. The American press has treated him as a sacred cow. . . . He has been praised in proportion to the very fine feats of detection which his bureau has achieved, and a little beyond, for the G-men have received entire credit for some jobs in which other agencies took part. He is a great personal press agent, and he has pet writers, or stooges, with access to big newspaper and magazine circulation, who scratch his back in return for material that glorifies J. Edgar Hoover and the G's.

Max Lowenthal's groundbreaking 1950 book *The Federal Bureau of Investigation* was the result of ten years of research. It is a damning document that quotes widely from Hoover's critics in and out of the government. Hoover applied pressure to keep the book from being published. He had Lowenthal called before the House Committee on Un-American Activities in an effort to discredit the book. The hearings were made public two days before the book's publication.

In the first thirty years of Hoover's reign, his critics were few. Their voices were drowned out by the praise heaped upon the director for his successful attacks against extremists, bank robbers, kidnappers, and spies.

But by the late 1950s and into the 1970s, Hoover began to be criticized by a growing number of authors, journalists, university professors, organizations, congressmen, former police commissioners, and ex-FBI agents. And their voices began to be heard.

The FBI's history, they claimed, was one of violating — rather than protecting — the principles America stood for. They accused Hoover of having deported people without due process early in his career, of arresting them without proper procedures. They questioned the G-Men's success against the bank robbers and kidnappers of the 1930s. Their notorious reputation, said Hoover's critics, had been artificially inflated by newspaper articles fed by the bureau's effective public relations department. The FBI's Ten Most Wanted fugitives was called by some a publicity gimmick. William Turner, a ten-year former FBI agent, said that "the . . . FBI Top Ten fugitives are for the most part human tumbleweeds of slight menace to society as a whole." Turner also agreed with those who said the FBI rarely gave other federal agencies and local police the credit they deserved:

> The famous Lady in Red who put the finger on Dillinger was an informant for the . . . Secret Service, not the FBI. . . . The Lindbergh kidnapper . . . was trapped by . . . Treasury agents, not the FBI. . . . The German saboteurs landed by submarine during World War II were betrayed by their own leader.

In 1964, Fred J. Cook's *The FBI Nobody Knows* told the real story of many of the FBI's supposed successes. Cook's book was widely read, and others joined the chorus. (Hoover tried to suppress its publication, also.)

Many questioned the conviction statistics Hoover quoted. He boasted that the FBI had a 98 percent rate of conviction. But as far back as 1937, there were those who doubted that was the case. In that year, the Senate authorized a study of all federal law enforcement agencies. The study found that the bureau had, in fact, a 72.5 percent conviction rate: a rate lower than that of the Narcotics Bureau, the Secret Service, the Post Office Inspection Service, and the IRS.

Hoover liked to explain precisely how much money the bureau was saving the country each year by recovering stolen vehicles. But most cars were recovered by local authorities who called the FBI as a matter of procedure. The bureau's reputation for working with the local police was not, it seemed, as productive as Hoover claimed. The FBI's relationship with the Los Angeles and New York police departments was a poor one. Other local agencies complained that the exchange of information went only one way. They supplied the information and the FBI took all of the credit.

Another statistic the bureau was proud of quoting was shown to be more myth than reality. In the 1930s, the FBI had indeed given preference to lawyers and accountants when hiring agents. During World War II, however, the bureau hired agents who did not have legal or accounting degrees. But these modifications were off the record. On the record, Hoover still claimed lawyers and accountants were given preference. But that was no longer the case by 1960. Less than one out of three agents were lawyers and slightly more than one in ten were accountants.

Critics argued that the FBI was preoccupied with compiling impressive statistics in order to maintain budget increases. While the FBI was looking for stolen cars in order to beef up the numbers, traffic in illegal narcotics increased.

The journalist Jack Anderson wrote:

> The FBI has plenty of agents to search for stolen cars, infiltrate antiwar rallies, keep files on Congressmen and polish J. Edgar Hoover's image. But it has assigned only four to the Justice Department's vital 17-city drive against the Mafia.

Some of the sharpest criticism was reserved for the FBI's role during the anti-communist 1950s. Senator Joseph McCarthy and the House Committee on Un-American Activities had accused and often hounded innocent people with information readily supplied by the FBI.

Critics agreed that the bureau was a disciplined and efficient organization, but they wondered at what cost. Hoover, they claimed, was obsessed with loyalty.

Patrick Murphy, a former police commissioner of New York City, said:

> I think he looked for someone who would conform, be willing to come into the FBI and do what he was told. Don't think independently. . . . This is not the kind of place for creativity or dissent, other than to be creative to make the Bureau look good and to make Mr. Hoover look good.

His elaborate system of inspections and his encouragement of agents to report on each other had led to an atmosphere of fear. A fear that existed all the way up to the executive level. Even William Sullivan, an assistant director, believed Hoover had tapped his phone. Sullivan used a pay phone for calls he considered confidential.

Hoover made sure that the FBI protected his reputation as much as it protected anything else. Field offices were instructed to clip articles critical of the director and send them to headquarters. Usually a file was opened on the article's author, who was then considered an enemy of the FBI. Hoover also ordered that all field office press releases begin with his name and mention him twice more in the text.

Hoover himself was considered something of a mystery. He had single-handedly created the world's best-known investigative agency. Yet, he never personally investigated a case, couldn't drive a car, and had never been instructed on how to fire a gun.

Some opponents said Hoover was a dictator, and that his men were terrorized by him. Hoover liked to scrawl messages in green ink in the margins of memos he received. Once he felt that the margins were too narrow, leaving too little room for him to say what he had to say. He wrote, "Watch the borders." And that's just what the FBI did: Both the Canadian and Mexican borders were watched for a week after that.

A former FBI agent, Ted Rosack, wrote:

> We had the dress code — no beards, no moustaches. You wore white shirts, striped ties, conservative suits, wingtip shoes and, in the early days, hats. . . . That was part of the discipline. It was just something you went along with. I didn't wear a blue shirt until after Hoover died.

Agents dreaded shaking Hoover's hand because they knew he considered a sweaty palm a sign of bad character. Personal appearances seemed to count for more than performance. One assistant director was forced to resign simply because he had hired a filing clerk who had pimples on his face. There was no dialogue and no debate within the FBI.

Hoover had created the bureau in his own image: white, male, and Christian; Americans who thought like Hoover, acted like Hoover, and did what Hoover told them.

Throughout his career, Hoover had powerful friends in Congress. But his critics began to include members of the Senate and the House. One of the FBI's sharpest critics, Congressman Don Edwards, was a former FBI agent. Bureau abuses in the areas of civil and constitutional rights concerned Edwards:

> Regardless of the unattractiveness or noisy militancy of some private citizens or organizations, the Constitution does not permit federal intervention with their activities except through the criminal justice system. . . . There are no exceptions. . . . It is the essence of freedom.

Other congressmen were concerned about the power that surrounded the director. They worried about all those files they had heard about, including files on members of Congress themselves. How much information did he have and on whom? Some feared that he would use those files if they crossed him. One Washington correspondent claimed there was enough material to "thoroughly embarrass half of America."

William C. Sullivan, a former FBI assistant director, called Hoover a "master blackmailer":

> The moment he would get something on a senator he would send one of his errand boys up and advise the senator they were in the course of an investigation and by chance happened to come up with this data. . . . But we wanted you to know this — we realized you'd want to know it. . . . What does that tell the senator? From that time on, the senator was right in his pocket.

Tom Wicker, one of the most respected journalists of his day, wrote a major article in *The New York Times Magazine*. The 1969 article was aptly titled, "What Have They Done Since They Shot Dillinger?" In it he wrote: "The Bureau is simply not as good or as impartial a law enforcement agency as it ought to be — certainly not as good as the myth suggests."

A growing number of critics believed that Hoover considered himself above the law. Hoover alone, they felt, chose where the bureau's manpower, resources, and investigative capabilities were focused. They feared that the bureau had become an independent arm of the government and they wondered just how independent it had become.

CHAPTER EIGHT

★

HOOVER AND THE KENNEDYS

"The three most overrated things in the world are the state of Texas, the FBI, and mounted deer heads."

President John F. Kennedy

John F. Kennedy was the first president younger than Hoover: twenty-three years younger. He was born the year Hoover took his first job as a clerk in the Justice Department. Kennedy's victory in the 1960 presidential election was considered a victory for youth. At his inauguration, Kennedy proclaimed that "the torch has been passed to a new generation of Americans, born in this century." That month, January, 1961, Hoover had turned sixty-six. He had been director of the FBI for thirty-six years.

J. Edgar Hoover and John F. Kennedy represented different ends of the American political spectrum. Hoover, although he never joined a political party, had supported Richard Nixon in his presidential race. Hoover had become a symbol of law and order. He stood for those who were on guard against the menace of communism and subversion: a threat he considered real and immediate. Hoover believed Kennedy underestimated the seriousness of that threat.

President Kennedy's priorities were different from Hoover's. He was concerned with the country's growing domestic problems. Crime, poverty, health, education, and race were all important issues on the new president's agenda. Communism, radicalism, spying, and disloyalty — things Hoover considered priorities — were not.

Kennedy had defeated then Vice President Richard Nixon by a narrow margin. Out of 68,832,818 votes counted, Kennedy had won by only 118,550. It was one of the closest presidential races in American history. One of Kennedy's first official announcements, the day after the election, was to ask J. Edgar Hoover to continue as director of the FBI. Most Kennedy supporters were surprised and disappointed. They had expected Hoover to be one of the first to go when the new administration took over.

Kennedy's decision to reappoint Hoover was largely a political one. He knew that Hoover had personal information about him in his files that could be embarrassing if made public. If the newly elected president was going to accomplish his goals, he would need the support of southern congressmen who were loyal to the director. Dismissing Hoover would create too many powerful enemies. Hoover would have to stay — at least for the first term. By then Hoover would have reached the mandatory retirement age of 70. The rumor was that the axe would then fall.

As if one Kennedy wasn't enough, the president-elect named his younger brother attorney general. As the head of the Justice Department, Robert Kennedy, thirty years younger than Hoover, would be his superior. The FBI tour guide began to inform visitors that "Mr. Hoover had become director of the bureau in 1924, the year before the attorney general was born." Kennedy put a stop to it as soon as he heard about it, but the message was clear.

Hoover's dislike for the Kennedys, particularly Robert, was profound. They clashed right from the start. It was, to some extent, a conflict of young versus old. But there was more to it than that.

President John F. Kennedy and his brother Robert, the Attorney General

Previously Hoover's power and prestige had permitted him to work directly with the president, but Robert Kennedy was unwilling to allow the director to go over his head. He saw to it that Hoover's calls to the White House were refused by the president's aides. Hoover, retaliating, became unavailable when the attorney general called him. Robert Kennedy responded by having a direct line installed. But Hoover didn't answer that phone, either. Losing patience one day, Kennedy told Helen Gandy, Hoover's loyal secretary of 43 years, "When I pick up this phone there's only one man I want to talk to — get the phone on the Director's desk."

Hoover favored formal meetings with assigned times. Kennedy's habit of dropping in on him irritated the director. The "Kennedy style" — shoes off, feet up, tie loosened, and sleeves rolled up — further annoyed Hoover. Some FBI agents privately ridiculed the touch-football games Robert Kennedy organized. Others referred to his office as "the playpen" partly because of the children's art that adorned the walls.

Robert Kennedy brought his dog and his children to the office occasionally, allowing them to run free in the halls of the Justice Department. Hoover, a lifetime government worker, considered the younger Kennedy's behavior disrespectful. Hoover suffered silently the humorous newspaper reports of the time:

ROUNDUP AT F.B.I.

J. Edgar Hoover, director of the Federal Bureau of Investigation, does not call many general staff meetings. But enough gangbusters came running to his office recently to plan a roundup of the first ten public enemies.

Attorney General Robert F. Kennedy was taking his children on a tour of the Justice Department when they ended up in the director's office. Mr. Hoover was away from his desk, below which the youngsters discovered a fascinating row of buttons. They did what came naturally, and before the grown-ups knew what had happened, two-thirds of the F.B.I. top command hurried through the door.

J. Edgar Hoover had a difficult relationship with the Kennedys. Bobby Kennedy's casual style especially infuriated him.

Robert Kennedy's people talked about Hoover behind Hoover's back. They commented on his moodiness, moodiness they associated with someone who had been doing the same job too long. One day he would be well-organized and efficient and the next he would be, as they put it, "out of it."

Rumors had it that Robert Kennedy suspected Hoover had had his office bugged. One day, discussing an issue with a staff member, Kennedy asked if the director knew about it. Looking at the ceiling, the staff member said, "I guess he does now." The attorney general stood up, placed his hands around his mouth and shouted at the ceiling, "Edgar, can you hear me, Edgar?"

Robert Kennedy and
J. Edgar Hoover

Hoover fought Kennedy's attempts to act like his boss. He even refused to attend staff luncheons called by the attorney general. Robert Kennedy wanted to have his own way, but he was unwilling to risk a public confrontation with the powerful director of the FBI.

The attorney general and the director conflicted sharply over issues of substance. Organized crime and racism within the FBI were two areas over which they clashed most heatedly.

ORGANIZED CRIME

Robert Kennedy wanted the bureau to operate within the policy guidelines established by the Justice Department. The attorney general had already made public his number one priority: organized crime. The FBI had only twelve agents assigned to organized crime. Over a thousand were involved in political security cases involving suspected antigovernment activity. Kennedy wanted to shift the bureau's resources away from these domestic-security cases and concentrate them on organized crime. Kennedy pressured Hoover to take a more aggressive role in fighting the Mafia.

By the 1940s, the Mafia had developed into a well-run, highly organized national crime syndicate. The Mafia had been able to take control of a wide variety of illegal activities in the United States, including gambling, trafficking in illegal drugs, extortion, loan-sharking (loaning money at illegal and excessively high interest rates), and murder, while the FBI was otherwise occupied.

The Mafia had never been a priority for Hoover. "No single individual, or coalition of racketeers, dominates organized crime across the country." But Hoover was wrong.

In 1957, a New York State police sergeant had discovered a Mafia meeting in the small upstate town of Apalachin. The conference of more than sixty gangland crime figures was a major news story across the country. The discovery of the gathering was considered proof that there was indeed an organized, national crime syndicate, but it did little to change Hoover's attitude.

A year after the Apalachin meeting, Hoover recalled an FBI report on organized crime. Twenty-five numbered copies had been circulated to government officials. Within twenty-four hours, Hoover had them retrieved and destroyed. He called the report "baloney." It is significant that, in 1959, the New York office had four agents assigned to organized crime, while four hundred agents investigated alleged communist activities.

The Kennedy administration's pressure on Hoover to do something about organized crime had intensified. The FBI's position seemed hopelessly out-of-date. Reluctantly, Hoover began to give in. But it was too late. Although the FBI had the manpower and it was within its jurisdiction, it had done very little to combat the rise of organized crime in the United States.

CIVIL RIGHTS

Race was another important policy area where the attorney general and the director differed.

J. Edgar Hoover was not sympathetic to the plight of America's black citizens. The schools and churches he had attended as a child were white, as was the neighborhood in which he spent his first forty-three years. (In 1938, when his mother died, he moved to Rock Creek Park, also a white area in DC.) In many ways the Washington, DC, that Hoover grew up in was a southern city. Separation of the races was the rule. The city's hotels, restaurants, and schools were all segregated.

Nearly all FBI agents were white. Hoover had made his black chauffeur and other personal employees agents, but that was just a technicality. A joke told by insiders was that there were two black FBI agents: "One took your coat and the other drove Hoover's car."

When Robert Kennedy wanted to recruit and hire more blacks to work in the FBI, Hoover refused to cooperate. When asked by the attorney general how many black agents there were, Hoover replied that the FBI did not catalogue employees by race, creed, or color. *Time* reported Hoover as saying, "Kennedy had wanted me to lower our qualifications and hire some more Negro agents. I said, 'Bobby, that's not going to be done as long as I am Director of this Bureau.' "

Hoover employed the tactics of evasion, delay, and when that failed, inaction. The attorney general grew annoyed and frustrated. His efforts to insure that the FBI did not discriminate were futile.

DALLAS

By the fall of 1963, President Kennedy was already turning his attention to the 1964 election. An impressive victory would allow him to take action in areas where he had been forced to proceed cautiously.

The president was looking forward to the upcoming campaign. He planned to visit the Texas cities of San Antonio, Houston, Fort Worth, and Dallas in late November. Vice President and Mrs. Johnson would be on the trip. After all, winning votes in LBJ's home state was one of the reasons why Kennedy had named the former Texas senator his vice-president. The big news, though, was that Mrs. Kennedy would be accompanying her husband on a presidential campaign trip for the first time.

On November 22, 1963, Lee Harvey Oswald was also in Dallas.

The president's Lincoln convertible was traveling at 11.2 mph as it negotiated the curves that ran past the Texas Book Depository Building. At 12:30 P.M., the president was hit by a bullet from Oswald's rifle. At 1:00, the CBS television network interrupted normal programming to announce: "From Dallas, Texas, this flash, apparently official: President Kennedy died at 1:00 P.M. Central Standard Time."

President Kennedy was assassinated in Dallas, Texas, on November 22, 1963.

Ironically, it was J. Edgar Hoover who first informed Robert Kennedy that his brother had been assassinated in Dallas. Later that same day, the attorney general called the director on the hot line he had insisted remain on Hoover's desk. It rang and rang. Finally Hoover told an aide, "Now get that phone back on Miss Gandy's desk."

From that time forward, Hoover went directly to Lyndon Baines Johnson, the new president. During the last six months of Robert Kennedy's tenure as attorney general, Hoover did not even speak to him.

CHAPTER NINE

★

HOOVER AND THE CIVIL RIGHTS MOVEMENT

"The FBI treated the civil rights movement as if it were an alien enemy attack on the United States."

Civil rights leader Coretta Scott King

"It's a shame that national concern is aroused only after two white boys are missing."

Civil rights leader John Lewis

The civil rights movement that blossomed in the 1950s had its origins hundreds of years earlier. In the 1600s, the first black Africans were forced into slavery in the American colonies. By 1750, there were 200,000 slaves on the cotton and tobacco plantations of the South (where slavery was concentrated.)

In 1793, the cotton gin was invented by Eli Whitney. This machine removed the seeds from the cotton fiber as fast as fifty people working by hand. More people were needed to pick the cotton now that it could be processed so much faster. The southern cotton industry expanded, as did slavery. By 1860, there were four million slaves toiling on southern plantations.

In 1863, President Abraham Lincoln issued the Emancipation Proclamation. This freed the slaves in the southern states that had rebelled, which had led to the Civil War (1861–1865). Two years later, in 1865, the Thirteenth Amendment to the Constitution ended slavery throughout the United States.

But in the years following the Civil War, black Americans continued to be treated as second-class citizens. Most of the approximately four million freed slaves had no homes, were poor, and could not read or write. Most southern whites resisted attempts by blacks to vote or hold office. Efforts by blacks to enjoy their civil rights were met by violence: Thousands of blacks were murdered in the South. Black churches and schools were burned, and segregation and discrimination continued. Many southern states passed laws that prohibited blacks from owning land. Other laws enforced separation by race on railway cars and led to the creation of separate drinking fountains and bathrooms. Many courts even used separate Bibles for swearing in black or white witnesses. In housing, education, employment, and public facilities (restaurants, hotels, and means of transportation, for example), black Americans were segregated from white Americans.

In the early 1900s, about a million southern blacks moved to cities in the North. Lacking the skills, experience, and education needed to find good jobs, they lived in rundown housing in crowded areas. Large, all-black slums developed in these big cities. These slums became known as ghettos.

In 1945, after World War II, the struggle for civil rights increased. Nearly a million blacks had served in the armed forces during that war. Returning veterans were less accepting of the injustices of the racial discrimination that they had fought against overseas. In addition, blacks in the North were insisting on improved education for their children and better jobs for themselves. Membership in the National Association for the Advancement of Colored People (NAACP) increased. The NAACP had been formed in 1909, and along with the new members came increased financial support. The NAACP used this money to launch legal battles against racially discriminating laws. The NAACP's legal campaign achieved a number of important victories. The most important was the 1954 U.S. Supreme Court ruling in the case of *Brown* v. *the Board of*

Education. This landmark decision said that Oliver Brown's eight-year-old daughter was being treated unfairly and illegally by not being allowed to attend a white public school in her neighborhood. Separation in education, said the Supreme Court, was unequal, and therefore illegal. It would no longer be tolerated. They ordered the integration of the nation's public schools to proceed "with all deliberate speed."

In the 1950s, following this ruling, the black struggle for civil rights intensified. In the fall of 1955, Emmett Till, a black child, was brutally murdered in Mississippi. The killing of the eighth-grader from Chicago (who was visiting relatives in Mississippi at the time) horrified the nation. The all-white jury deliberated only an hour and seven minutes before deciding that the two white men on trial were not guilty. This case further illustrated the serious nature of the racial problem in the United States. Three months after Emmett Till's murder, the Montgomery bus boycott began.

In 1955, it was illegal for black people to sit in seats reserved for whites. This was the way things were in Alabama and in most of the South. If the seats in the white section were filled and more whites boarded the bus, then some black passengers would have to stand.

On December 1, 1955, Rosa Parks, a seamstress and the secretary of the local NAACP chapter, refused to give up her seat for a white person. "I had decided that I would have to know once and for all what rights I had as a human being and citizen," Ms. Parks said. Her refusal sparked a 382-day struggle in Montgomery, Alabama.

Blacks organized a boycott of the city's buses. By not using the buses, blacks were hurting the city financially. It became a question of who would give in first.

Reverend Martin Luther King, Jr., was twenty-six when he was asked to coordinate Montgomery's boycott efforts. He was the minister of the Dexter Avenue Baptist Church. When the boycott was over, Martin Luther King, Jr., emerged as a nationally recognized black leader.

Black Americans took refuge from a white mob in this Montgomery, Alabama, church.

The Reverend Dr. Martin Luther King, Jr., led the successful boycott against the segregated Montgomery bus system.

The year-long strike against the city's buses was successful: The city abolished the unjust bus law. The black citizens of Montgomery, Alabama, had proved that there were peaceful, but forceful steps that could be taken to obtain equal treatment.

With sixty other black ministers, Dr. King formed the Southern Christian Leadership Conference (SCLC) in 1957, and was elected its first president. The SCLC became one of the country's strongest and most influential civil rights organizations.

Dr. King taught that unjust laws should be resisted, but without violence. He believed that hate should be returned with love. He preached:

"There is some good in the worst of us and some evil in the best of us
. . . each of us is two selves. And the great burden of life is to always
try to keep that higher self in command."

He organized and led boycotts, sit-ins, and marches. He allowed himself to be arrested and carried off to jail as a protest against the injustices
suffered by American blacks.

J. Edgar Hoover believed that the civil rights movement was being
influenced secretly by the communists, that agents of the Soviet Union
were using the civil rights movement to try to destroy the United States
government. Hoover believed that the civil rights movement was neither
spontaneous nor genuine, so in 1958, the FBI began watching Dr. King.
Three years later, Hoover decided that watching wasn't enough. The

A civil rights demonstrator demands equal rights — NOW!

The civil rights movement gained force and influence from the mid 1950s through the early 1960s.

bureau began an investigation. That investigation convinced Hoover that one of King's closest advisors had been associated with the Communist party of the United States. Hoover was further convinced that Stanley Levison, a white lawyer, *still* had ties to the communists.

A complex relationship between Hoover, the Kennedys, and King developed. Hoover attempted to convince the president that King was being influenced by the communists because of his association with Levison. President Kennedy was concerned about what would happen if Hoover's information became available to the news media. It would, he felt, do serious damage to the civil rights movement. Not only might people begin to doubt the movement's goals, but Congress would grow suspicious, and even more reluctant to enact legislation.

In late June, 1963, the president spoke with Dr. King while walking in the White House Rose Garden. The president pressed King to end his contact with people in his organization who were thought to be associated with the communists. King asked the president if he had any proof of this association. Kennedy stressed that it sometimes didn't matter if things like this were true or not. Even a rumor of communist affiliations within the civil rights movement might be enough to cause considerable trouble. The president strongly urged Dr. King to take care of the matter.

The conversation with Kennedy disturbed King. He felt torn. He had no doubts that his friend Stanley Levison was sincere. But he knew that the president was right. All too often, rumor had a force equal to that of truth — especially when it came to politics.

Stanley Levison and Martin Luther King, Jr., agreed to cease all direct communication. They did, however, continue to communicate through a third party. And the FBI continued to monitor these conversations.

The phones in the New York and Atlanta offices of the SCLC, as well as Dr. King's home phone, were tapped. To Hoover, the country's na-

Robert Kennedy
and Dr. Martin
Luther King, Jr., in
Washington, DC

tional security was at stake. Dr. King's name was placed on the Emergency Detention List. This was a list of people who were to be arrested in the event of hostilities with certain foreign countries.

Earlier, in an article in *The Nation*, King called for the end of racial discrimination in federal employment. Then, in the fall of 1962, he told a reporter for *The New York Times* that "one of the great problems we [the civil rights movement] face with the FBI agents in the South is that the agents are white southerners who have to be friendly with the local police who are promoting segregation." By criticizing the bureau publicly, King had violated one of Hoover's sacred rules. Hoover's dislike for King became even more intense.

By the fall of 1963, the civil rights movement had become the most important issue in the country.

MIBURN: MISSISSIPPI BURNING

Hoover's conflict with the civil rights movement was not limited to the activities of Dr. Martin Luther King, Jr. The bureau was the object of criticism from other civil rights leaders because FBI agents were unwilling to come to the aid of southern blacks.

Hoover, aside from any personal feelings he had, was reluctant to become involved in civil rights cases for three reasons.

First, civil rights violations were difficult to prove in court. The chances of conviction were slim and the process leading to trial was lengthy and complicated. Since 1947, 1,570 civil rights cases in federal courts had resulted in only 27 convictions, according to Hoover. The director was proud of the bureau's conviction rate. Civil rights cases were sure to hurt that rate — and that could affect the bureau's budget.

The second reason was the relationship between an FBI agent and local police. That relationship was expected to be an excellent one. Often the FBI agent knew and liked the local sheriff, his deputies, and the mayor. They considered the local police brothers-in-arms fighting the same war against crime. The civil rights movement turned that relationship upside down. The federal agent was now asked to view the local police as law *breakers* — not law enforcers. In many civil rights cases, it was the local authorities who were illegally denying law-abiding citizens their civil rights. Now *they* were the ones who were to be watched, wiretapped, tracked down, and even arrested. This kind of thinking did not come easily to the FBI agents. They were not accustomed to treating the local authorities as potential targets of criminal investigations. FBI agents expressed doubts that they could ask the local police for help to solve a crime one minute, and investigate them the next.

The bureau had a system of office preference assignments. Agents could choose where they wanted to work, and often worked near their own hometowns. Southern agents often ended up working in the South. In most cases they differed very little from their neighbors. Often they shared their negative feelings about the civil rights demonstrators. As one Mississippi police chief put it: "The FBI comes in here every day and we have coffee every day. We're very good friends."

The third reason was Hoover's longtime relationship with Democratic congressmen from the South. They had been backing Hoover and the bureau for years. Most of them, like Hoover, felt that the civil rights movement was made up of troublemakers and communists. The congressmen were happy with Hoover's decision that the FBI would be there watching from the sidelines.

But those involved in the civil rights movement could not accept the FBI's position. They wanted the bureau to use the same skills it used to end civil rights violations that it used to solve more complicated crimes. The FBI represented the concern of the federal government. Its presence would mean that the government of the United States believed that an injustice was being done. In the past, the FBI protected citizens from political radicals, gangsters, kidnappers, and spies. If violating someone's civil rights was a crime, why wasn't the FBI involved?

The FBI continued to stand on the sidelines, with the exception of one case in the summer of 1964. Three civil rights volunteers disappeared while working in Mississippi. The disappearance occurred a few days after a black church had been burned down by a group of white men. The case was code-named MIBURN — for Mississippi Burning — and it showed the bureau of the 1960s at its worst and at its best.

FREEDOM SUMMER

In the summer of 1964, civil rights leaders were planning to use student volunteers to work in Mississippi in a program called Freedom Summer. College students from across the country came to help Mississippi's black citizens register to vote.

Mississippi was considered the most segregated state in the country. It had the highest percentage of blacks and the lowest percentage of registered black voters. Only six percent of its black population of almost a million were eligible to vote. Some blacks in Mississippi had never even heard of voting.

Civil rights workers in Mississippi

Civil rights leaders wanted to concentrate their efforts in Mississippi precisely because of its racist reputation. They felt that if they could show progress in Mississippi, it would prove that progress could be made anywhere in the South. A successful Freedom Summer would be a significant step on the road to equality.

Student volunteers were given a crash course in Mississippi survival. They were taught what to do while being beaten by policemen with clubs. They were also instructed what *not* to do: for example, don't drive alone in a car or sleep by an open window. And, they were told, there was a good chance someone would be killed before it was all over.

Mississippi's white residents resented the outsiders who were invading their state. In Jackson, the state capital, the size of the police force had been doubled. The local paper said that outside agitators who "come in here and try to stir up trouble should be dealt with in a manner they won't forget."

THE KU KLUX KLAN

Civil rights leaders weren't the only ones active in the state of Mississippi during the summer of 1964. The Ku Klux Klan, with its increasing membership, was also planning its strategy.

The Ku Klux Klan was a secret organization that was started in Tennessee shortly after the Civil War. The Invisible Empire, as it was sometimes called, opposed the efforts of blacks, Catholics, and Jews to assimilate into American society. Early Klan members liked the scary sound of their meaningless name. They gave themselves exotic-sounding titles: Imperial Wizard, Grand Dragon, and Exalted Cyclops. Draped in sheets and wearing pillowcases for hoods, they began to terrify the recently freed black population. The Klansmen did their best to frighten them so they wouldn't use their newly acquired right to vote. They hoped that the blacks would think of them as "ghosts of the Confederate dead."

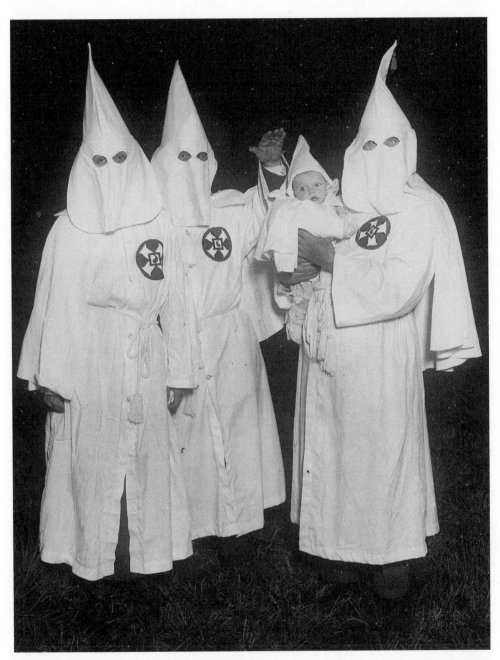

Ku Klux Klan members

Klan membership peaked in the early 1920s when there were an estimated four million members. (This was partly due to *Birth of a Nation*, a movie which was based on a novel titled *The Clansman*.) In 1925, 50,000 Klansmen, wearing their ceremonial robes and hoods, marched in Washington, DC, in a show of strength.

Membership fell after that until the early 1960s. The surge in Klan membership was due, in large part, to the activities of the civil rights movement.

Another important reason was the election of a Catholic president.

Although there was no central headquarters, regional chapters multiplied. One regional Klan organization was in Mississippi. Founded in 1964, it was called the White Knights of the Ku Klux Klan. Within a year, statewide membership had reached 5,000.

SCHWERNER, CHANEY, AND GOODMAN

Michael Schwerner, known as Mickey, turned 25 in 1964. Born and raised in New York City, he was a social worker. His wife Rita also worked helping the poor. Schwerner was one of hundreds of white college students working in Mississippi that summer. He believed that the struggle for equal rights was important and he felt he should be involved.

Mickey accepted the task of setting up a community center in Meridian, Mississippi. It was a particularly dangerous assignment, and it was the first time civil rights workers had been stationed outside of Jackson, the state capital.

In late January, 1964, Mickey and Rita set up headquarters in Meridian. They lived on the second floor above a black-owned drugstore. By the end of February, the community center was opened. There was a library with books on black history, a homemade Ping-Pong table, and a record player. Mickey gave evening instruction on how to register to vote.

Mickey was looked upon with scorn by the whites in the area. They warned him to stop what he was doing. The local police brought him in for questioning once a week.

Mickey was joined by 21-year-old James Chaney, a full-time civil rights worker. Chaney, a black man, had lived in Meridian all his life; he became Mickey's closest coworker.

On June 20, Schwerner and Chaney were joined by Andrew Goodman. Like Schwerner, Goodman was white and from New York City. He had arrived in Mississippi the day before. All three had just returned from Oxford, Ohio, after a training session for summer volunteers. When they got back that evening, they heard that a white mob had destroyed a 65-year-old church 35 miles from Meridian. Many of the church members

Andrew Goodman (*right*) at a training session for civil rights workers

were the people Mickey Schwerner was trying to help. There was more bad news: The men who had burned down the church had come looking for Mickey.

The three men drove out to visit the site of the fire the next day, Sunday, June 21, 1964. And then they disappeared.

THE INVESTIGATION

The FBI did not have a field office in Mississippi. Resident agents, as they were called, were responsible for bureau functions in the state. They worked out of their homes or used desks in federal buildings for offices. The six resident agents in the northern half of Mississippi reported to the Memphis, Tennessee, field office. The seven resident agents in southern Mississippi reported to the New Orleans, Louisiana, field office. Mississippi's resident agents spent their time tracking down stolen cars, investigating crimes committed on Indian reservations, and finding fugitives from justice. John Proctor had been an FBI agent for twelve years, the past one-and-a-half based in Meridian.

Proctor considered the investigation of the burning of the church routine. (More than twenty black churches would be firebombed in Mississippi that year.) When he was called about the disappearance of the three civil rights workers, he said he had no authority to act. This came as no surprise, as civil rights workers knew that they could not rely on the FBI to help them if they got into trouble.

Proctor was friendly with all the law-enforcement agents in the area, however, he did question Sheriff Lawrence Rainey and Deputy Sheriff Cecil Price. He wanted to know if they knew anything about the three missing volunteers.

He learned that Schwerner, Chaney, and Goodman had been arrested for speeding by Deputy Price. According to the sheriff, they were released from jail five hours later. They hadn't been heard from since.

Attorney General Robert Kennedy ordered that the case be treated as a kidnapping, invoking the "Lindbergh Law." The FBI now had responsibility for finding the missing civil rights workers. MIBURN had begun.

The FBI agent in charge of the New Orleans field office told Proctor he was sending five additional agents to Meridian. Major case inspector Joseph Sullivan was also sent to Meridian. The six-foot-two-inch Sullivan was a no-nonsense agent known for his thoroughness. Unlike most FBI agents, Sullivan was known to get involved in civil rights conflicts. During one demonstration, in Louisiana, he had publicly reprimanded the local police for not doing their job. As one bureau executive put it, Sullivan

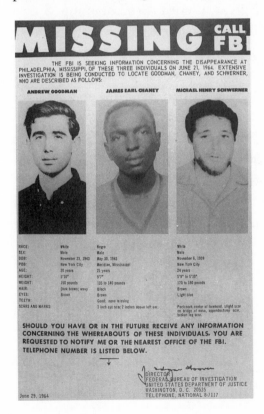

The FBI entered the Mississippi Burning case.

was "absolutely the best there was. If ever I did anything wrong, the last man in the world I would want after me was Joe Sullivan."

Sullivan had been ordered to Mississippi in early June. He had been asked to determine the seriousness of potential violence by the Ku Klux Klan, and the bureau's capabilities to deal with it properly.

Just after the FBI entered the case, Maynard King, a State Highway Patrol Inspector, gave Proctor a list of seven names, saying, "I have no proof, but I bet you every one of these men was involved in this." Sheriff Rainey and Deputy Price were on the list provided by Inspector King. Proctor's cultivation of local contacts was beginning to pay off.

In late June, Proctor received a phone call promising him something that the caller insisted would be of great interest. Proctor jumped into his car and sped off. Witnesses said they knew something was up because Proctor was driving so fast that the car's long police antenna was "laying all the way flat back." When he arrived, he was shown a car eight feet off the side of the highway, badly burned, stripped, and sunk in a swamp. There were no bodies and there was no evidence.

The discovery of the car made front-page news across the country. It heightened interest in what was already a national news story. Mississippi authorities were making no attempt to find the three missing civil rights workers and the pressure was on the FBI. Newsmen arrived from all over the country. Each day it became more unlikely that any of the three were alive. The FBI admitted that they were looking for the bodies.

Sullivan wouldn't allow the local authorities, especially the sheriff and his deputy, near the car. They didn't like it, but there wasn't anything they could do about it. Sullivan was intent upon proceeding with his investigation and there wasn't anything or anyone that was going to stand in his way.

J. Edgar Hoover, responding to pressure from President Johnson, announced the opening of an FBI field office in Jackson, the state capital.

The missing civil rights workers' car being pulled from a swamp

(Both Johnson and Hoover acted because of public pressure. At the president's request, Hoover even agreed to fly down to Jackson for the opening of the field office).

On July 5, Roy K. Moore, the FBI agent who was to be in charge of the new office, arrived in Mississippi. Moore, like Sullivan, had an outstanding reputation. He was respected by agents who had worked with him and for him and was known as someone who would stand up for them when necessary. Tough, but smooth, the forty-nine-year-old former

Marine could bend the rules if needed and had worked on the bureau's toughest cases for over twenty-six years. In 1955, he had played a critical role in solving the Denver commercial airline crash. Moore had taken charge of the FBI's investigation of the September, 1963, bombing of a Birmingham, Alabama, church that killed four girls ages eleven to fourteen (Code-named BAPBOMB).

Although a favorite agent of Hoover, Moore also had a reputation for disagreeing with the director when he felt it was necessary. (There were rumors that kept Moore from becoming an assistant director.)

Hoover was scheduled to arrive in Jackson on July 10. The office wasn't ready, and Moore persuaded an old friend to lease the top three floors of the First Federal Savings and Loan Building to the FBI. Hastily, Moore had a "temporary" office constructed in time for the ribbon-cutting ceremony. The photo opportunity went off without a hitch, and Hoover introduced Moore at a news conference held against the backdrop of the dummy office.

Some agents refused to be assigned to Jackson. They resigned rather than face the hostility of the white community and the danger it implied. Others volunteered. MIBURN was one of the most difficult FBI cases in years and the danger was a challenge to be met, not shied away from. Working with Moore was considered prestigious and exciting. Some agents volunteered because they felt it was their duty to show that the FBI could be an impartial and dedicated federal agency, one that would safeguard the rights of blacks as well as the security of banks.

Moore was Sullivan's superior, but it was Sullivan who ran the daily field investigation.

He organized search parties, using sailors from a nearby naval base. The Navy had offered the sailors and Hoover had approved. Four hundred sailors arrived in buses and joined the one hundred fifty-three FBI agents who had been sent to help locate the missing three.

They began searching the swamp where the car had been found. They tucked their pants legs into their shoes and used sticks to ward off deadly water moccasins and rattlesnakes. They found nothing.

There were rumors in Mississippi that the civil rights workers had staged the disappearance for publicity. Sheriff Rainey's opinion was: "If they're missing, they hid somewhere trying to get a lot of publicity out of it. . . . They're around somewhere laughing."

The pressure on the FBI increased daily. Director Hoover told reporters he believed that the three were dead. FBI agents had been instructed to continue the search until they were found. "The investigation is intensively being carried on. This may be a prolonged effort, but it will be continued until it is solved, until we find the bodies of those three men that have disappeared and the person who may be responsible for their disappearance."

There were so many FBI agents in the area that they had to set up temporary headquarters in a motel. Network television was showing news specials on the progress of the search. But Sullivan was convinced that they would never find the bodies by searching. The only way they would find the bodies was if someone would talk.

Sullivan believed that he could make someone connected with the crime talk. The atmosphere in the county was tense, the weather hot and humid. The townspeople were outwardly hostile as the FBI conducted their interviews and the newspaper people hung around.

In mid-July, Sullivan learned of a black teenager who had also been arrested by Sheriff Rainey. Rainey had released Wilmer Jones into the custody of a group of armed white men. They drove him around, asked him about his civil rights activities, and threatened to kill him. Miraculously, Jones was eventually set free. He agreed to help the FBI. Sullivan suspected that Schwerner, Chaney, and Goodman might have been taken to the same area Jones had been taken to. FBI agents drove Jones all

Dr. King speaks to a rally in Chicago, in front of portraits of the three dead civil rights workers.

over. When another car came near, he ducked. At times, a paper bag was placed over his head to prevent anyone from knowing who he was. The FBI believed he would be killed if seen.

Sullivan ordered his agents to focus their search on the area identified by Jones. To add pressure, the FBI offered a reward to anyone who could tell them where the bodies were buried. The FBI spread the word that as much as $30,000 would be given in exchange for the location of the graves. No information on who had committed the crime was necessary to collect the reward. As one high-level FBI memo put it: "The FBI is interested in but one thing at this time and that [is] to find the victims."

It was a tempting offer. In Mississippi, in 1964, $30,000 was a lot of money, and the informer just had to name the place where the men were buried.

"ONE WB"

On July 31, there was a major break in the case. Sullivan learned where the bodies of the three civil rights workers were buried. Sullivan did not meet directly with the informant, only with an intermediary. The FBI refused to name the source even when asked by the attorney general. "I could not identify the source of our information. . . . If we did, the source would be immediately killed," an FBI official stated. There was speculation that State Highway Patrol Inspector King might have been the person who told the FBI where the bodies were buried. But the name of the source is a closely held secret to this day.

The informant directed the FBI to a dam construction project on a nearby farm. Sullivan ordered agents to interview Sheriff Rainey and others again so that he and a team of agents could quietly head to the site.

They had difficulty finding the dam and enlisted the help of the Meridian Naval Air Station. With directions from the air, FBI agents were able to locate the dam.

The dam was 547 feet long, 83 feet thick, and about 20 feet high. Heavy equipment was brought in at dawn on August 4. A Caterpillar bulldozer with a ten-foot blade and a shovel that was suspended from a thirty-foot crane boom began digging. It was 106 degrees. Agents used garden tools and their bare hands to carefully sift through the dirt unearthed by the huge machines.

The information given to Sullivan proved accurate. At 3:18 P.M., "One WB" (white body) was found. They had found the first of the three missing civil rights workers. The other two were found soon after. The victims' families were notified, and an official announcement was made. It had been five weeks since they had disappeared.

The bullets removed from their bodies during the autopsies were sent for analysis to the FBI lab in Washington, DC. Based on microscopic scratches found on the bullets, they concluded that one gun had been used to shoot all three men. Traces of gunpowder indicated that they had been shot at close range.

Now that the bodies had been discovered, the Klansmen became visibly nervous. It was obvious that someone had told Sullivan where to look. Someone was talking to the FBI. But who? Mistrust slowly replaced the arrogance that had prevailed until then.

Sullivan and his agents did their best to increase the fear that was building among the Klansmen. Sullivan was betting that, eventually, the fear of being informed on would cause one of them to turn informer. Sullivan still had to know precisely what had happened. How did the three die? Who did it? He needed evidence. He needed an eyewitness to the crime.

The already tense atmosphere heightened as FBI agents intensified their tactics. A thousand Mississippi residents were interviewed, including every known Klan member in the area. "I had our agents interview every member of the Klan there, just to let them know we know who they are," Hoover stated.

FBI interviews of the Klansmen got rougher. Agents revealed their knowledge of one Klansman's secret number to show him how much they already knew. One agent parked his car all day in front of a Klansman's house. That way the Klansman's friends would think that he was talking to the FBI. It rattled the Klansman, and kept his friends away.

The town looked like it had been invaded by an enemy army and the townspeople acted that way. (There were now 250 FBI agents working on the case.) Sullivan believed that "fear of the Klan overlay the uncooperative attitude of some. Others perceived that the civil rights workers were outside troublemakers who had received their just dues. . . . The [Klan] owned the place. In spirit, everyone belonged to the Klan." Moore agreed, although he put it differently: "The difference here is that these people who commit racial crimes think they are on a religious mission. They don't consider themselves criminals." Agents carried around candy to get children to talk. The children revealed information about the comings and goings of their elders.

Finally, in late October, one Klansman broke down. And then another. The FBI agent who was conducting one of the interviews took forty pages of notes. By late November, the FBI had the whole story.

Samuel Bowers, the Imperial Wizard of the White Knights of the Ku Klux Klan, had ordered the "elimination" of Mickey Schwerner. Schwerner's execution was to be a bloody message to civil rights workers to stay out of the state of Mississippi.

On the night of June 16, 1964, members of the White Knights went to the Mount Zion Methodist Church to find and kill Mickey Schwerner. Unable to find him, they terrorized the black churchgoers, beat two, and set fire to the church.

After Schwerner, Goodman, and Chaney had visited the burned church, they were stopped by the police, arrested for speeding, and taken into custody. Schwerner asked to make a call. He wanted to let someone know where he was. (This was a safety precaution he had been taught. If someone knew where you were, there was less likelihood of any harm coming to you.) Schwerner was not allowed to make the call.

Shortly after the three were "released" from jail, they were turned over to the Klan. Within five minutes, all three had been "eliminated" by Klansmen wearing rubber gloves to prevent fingerprints. They were taken to the prearranged burial site, and their car was taken to be burned and destroyed.

A FEDERAL CASE

On the morning of December 4, 1964, FBI agents swarmed through the area and arrested Sheriff Rainey, Deputy Sheriff Price, and seventeen other members of the White Knights of the Ku Klux Klan. Agent Moore met with Mississippi state officials to determine possible legal action. It was clear that there was little likelihood that the state of Mississippi would bring any charges against any of the nineteen Klansmen. Murder is not a federal crime. Murder charges must be brought by the state. If the federal government did not bring charges, there would be no case and all nineteen would have to be released.

With the two confessions in hand, the true story of what had happened was known to the FBI. Justice Department lawyers who would try the case believed the FBI had obtained enough evidence to allow them to prosecute. Deciding what federal law to try the defendents under was an important and complicated legal question. The Justice Department decided to try the case using federal statutes that were nearly a century old.

The Civil Rights Act of 1866 and the Enforcement Act of 1870 had been passed during a period in American history known as the Reconstruction Era. This was a period of approximately ten years (until 1877) following the end of the Civil War. For the first time in American history, black Americans, most of whom had been slaves or the descendants of slaves, were free. The war had been won, but the many battles were not yet over.

Many southern states passed laws designed to limit the ability of black Americans to exercise their newly won rights. The federal government was forced into the role of protecting the civil rights of black Americans. A hundred years later this struggle continued.

It was difficult, if not impossible, for blacks in Mississippi to enjoy such a basic civil right as the right to vote. Laws were passed specifically to make it difficult for blacks to vote. One Mississippi law required that voters interpret portions of the state constitution before registering to vote. Another law required that the names of new voters be published in the newspaper for two weeks before the application could be approved. Such laws were enacted in order to intimidate and to prevent blacks from voting.

To prevent abuses of this and other civil rights, the federal government looked to the rights granted by these Reconstruction Era statutes to bring legal action.

Title 18, Section 241 of the U.S. Criminal Code was part of the Civil Rights Act of 1870. It made it unlawful for two or more persons to "conspire to injure, oppress, threaten, or intimidate any citizen in the free exercise or enjoyment of any right or privilege secured to him by the Constitution or the laws of the United States." Section 241 provided for a maximum sentence of ten years in jail and a five-thousand-dollar fine.

The Justice Department, relying on the comprehensive FBI investigation (MIBURN resulted in 150,000 pages by the time the case was closed), would attempt to prove that the nineteen Klansmen had participated in a conspiracy to deprive the three civil rights workers of their constitutional right to register voters in the state of Mississippi.

There had been but one successful criminal prosecution of a federal civil rights case in almost twenty years. And *that* case had eventually been overturned. The Justice Department knew they were taking on a difficult task.

In January, 1965, indictments were handed down by a federal grand jury against the nineteen defendants. One month later, William Harold Cox, a federal judge of the South District of Mississippi threw out the case. Thirteen months later, in March, 1966, the U.S. Supreme Court overruled Cox, and one year after that, in February, 1967, the nineteen were reindicted. On October 20, 1967, with Judge Cox presiding, the "Western Division Criminal Action number 5291, United States of America, plaintiff, versus Cecil Ray Price, et al., defendants" case was concluded when an all-white jury found seven of the defendants guilty.

It was the first time a Mississippi jury had convicted white officials and Klansmen for crimes against blacks and civil rights workers.

On December 26, 1967, two of the defendants were sentenced to the maximum term of ten years; two received six years; and three received three years. Sheriff Rainey had been found not guilty.

Years after the trial, Judge Cox had this to say about the sentences: "They killed one nigger, one Jew, and a white man. I gave them what I thought they deserved."

Their appeals were denied and they began serving their sentences in March, 1970. All were paroled before serving their full prison terms, and most had returned to the area by the mid-1970s.

Neither the state of Mississippi nor the county in which the crimes had been committed have ever conducted an investigation into these murders and no charges have ever been brought by them.

THE CAMPAIGN AGAINST KING

During the MIBURN investigation, Hoover continued his aggressive investigation of Dr. Martin Luther King, Jr. Steps were taken by the FBI to confuse and disrupt the civil rights leader, hopefully affecting his ability to lead. Hoover wanted to gather evidence that would show that King was using the movement for personal gain. Hoover's goal was to force King to leave the national political scene. Hoover and his assistants even went so far as to choose the names of suitable replacements.

Hoover had become obsessed with King. It was said that it was hard to talk to him about anything else. Hoover had the FBI pursue King without letup. When King traveled, which he did often, his hotel room was bugged. The rooms of those traveling with him were also bugged.

The bugs yielded little. Either by chance or because King and his group suspected something, their TV was so loud that it was often difficult to hear exactly what was being said. But they did hear some things. Nothing about politics or communist connections. But embarrassing things were recorded about Dr. King's personal life. Hoover had "highlight" tapes made and circulated them among the FBI's friends in Congress and the media.

In October, 1964, much to Hoover's disbelief, Dr. Martin Luther King, Jr., was chosen to receive the Nobel Peace Prize. In 1963, he had been named "Man of the Year" by *Time*. Hoover could no longer keep his outrage private.

In November, 1964, speaking at a press conference of Washington newspaperwomen, Hoover called King the "most notorious liar" and "one of the lowest characters in the country." Hoover's remarks made national headlines.

Hoover was reacting to King's statement in 1962 that FBI agents were often southern born and incapable of viewing blacks impartially. King's criticism of the FBI continued as the civil rights movement's activities continued. In 1964, he said that civil rights workers were not bothering to report violations because FBI agents were prejudiced. DR. KING SAYS FBI FAVORS SEGREGATIONISTS, quoted *The New York Times*. The *Times* soon ran an editorial called "Time to Retire." The editorial wondered if the director shouldn't retire when he turned 70 in January. (Seventy was the mandatory retirement age, but President Johnson had already issued an executive order that would allow Hoover to continue for an indefinite period of time.)

In December, a meeting was arranged between Hoover and King. The 55-minute meeting solved nothing. Both sides reported what happened differently. But in each case there was very little to report.

Martin Luther King, Jr., leaving J. Edgar Hoover's office. Hoover had called King, "the most notorious liar in the country."

Things continued very much as before.

King was feeling harassed by the FBI. Unknown to him, the bureau had successfully placed an undercover agent within the Southern Christian Leadership Conference. The agent reported weekly to his FBI superior. King, suspicious but not knowing completely what was going on, became deeply disturbed by the situation.

In 1968, King went to Memphis, Tennessee, where the city's sanitation workers (almost all black) were striking. The atmosphere was heated and tense. Violence had erupted between police and marchers. One march had already ended in a riot, with one marcher dead. Dr. King was frustrated by his inability to bring order to the situation. On April 4, he had an afternoon meeting to discuss a rift within the Memphis black leadership. After the meeting, Dr. King and others were planning to leave for dinner. When he stepped out onto the balcony of the motel where he was staying, he was killed by an assassin's bullet.

"Oh God, when is all this violence going to stop?" Robert Kennedy cried out when told that Dr. King had been shot.

Kennedy, by then a senator from New York, was a candidate for the 1968 Democratic presidential nomination. On the evening of June 5, 1968, Senator Kennedy gave a victory speech after defeating Senator Eugene McCarthy in the critical California primary. Following his speech, he took a detour through the hotel kitchen, where he was shot by a man standing among the workers.

On the day of Robert Kennedy's funeral, James Earl Ray, who was believed to be the man who killed Dr. Martin Luther King, Jr., was captured in London's Heathrow Airport. Hoover ordered the news of Ray's capture delayed several hours so that the announcement would interrupt live television coverage of the former attorney general's funeral.

CHAPTER TEN

★

COINTELPRO: THE FBI'S <u>CO</u>UNTER <u>INTELLIGENCE PR</u>OGRAM

"It's hard for me to believe that the FBI, which I have revered for many years, has fallen to that low an estate."

US District Court Judge Fred Nichol

By the mid-1960s, the struggle for civil rights had shifted north. New York, Washington, Philadelphia, Detroit, Chicago, Boston, Los Angeles, and other cities were plagued by rioting, looting, arson, and other violence.

Blacks had become impatient with the tactics of nonviolent protest, voter registration drives, school desegregation confrontations, and the pressuring of white political leaders. The voices of new black leaders were being heard and new black organizations, considered radical by most, were attracting members. Although none were able to attract the mass support that Dr. Martin Luther King, Jr., could call on, they did appeal to many blacks, especially those living in urban ghettos. Some of the black leaders emerging in the mid- and late-1960s advocated the use of force and weapons in self-defense, rather than nonviolence. They were calling for blacks to stand up and revolt against their white oppressors. Now was the time of "Black Power." No longer content to ask for what was rightly theirs, blacks were demanding it.

Many white Americans feared that the random violence that seemed to be occurring every summer night might spread. They were demanding that law and order be preserved. Black leaders cried "Burn, baby, burn" while the nation's cities seemed to be doing just that.

The nation's leaders were concerned about the explosive situation. President Johnson turned to the FBI, and Hoover responded. He had already begun preparing the bureau to combat yet another threat to the security of the country.

Hoover considered all black power groups extreme, so extreme tactics were called for. Hoover decided to implement COINTELPRO.

COINTELPRO was the code name for <u>C</u>ounter <u>I</u>ntelligence <u>P</u>rogram. Counterintelligence meant that action would be taken to weaken these organizations.

A young man gives the black power salute.

Hoover wanted to stop these groups from forming coalitions and building memberships. He wanted to destroy them before they could become formidable. He also wanted to insure that a charismatic leader like King did not emerge. To do this, Hoover decided that the FBI would act not only as an investigative agency, but as a counterforce.

Convinced that these groups were out to harm the nation, Hoover set out to destroy them. The tactics that characterized COINTELPRO were the most extreme in the bureau's history. The use of these tactics marked a radical and major change in FBI methods.

COINTELPRO was designed to "divide, conquer, and weaken." The director stated that "the purpose of this new counterintelligence endeavor is to expose, disrupt, misdirect, or otherwise neutralize the activities of black nationalist . . . organizations."

FBI agents in the field were directed to take steps that would cause members of black radical groups to become fearful, mistrustful of one another, and confused. Agents were directed to exploit *all* avenues that might accomplish this and to recommend ideas.

There was long-term surveillance of members of these groups. Their home and office phones were tapped and their mail was opened without their knowledge. Offices were burglarized, and things were stolen, or planted or both.

The FBI sometimes sent fabricated letters to leaders of these organizations. They contained information designed to cause rifts in the leadership. It was hoped that these letters would create serious disagreements that would then waste the organization's time and energy. Effective leadership would become impossible because of the disagreements. Eventually, with their leaders' mistrust of each other, the organization would become unable to function. Sometimes these letters were designed to cause violence between group leaders. Letters might, in extreme cases, result in leaders killing each other off.

A Black Panther meeting in Chicago, Illinois. Hoover believed that the Panthers were a threat to the nation's security and began COINTELPRO to fight them.

Letters and leaflets were writted by the FBI and distributed as if they were written by one of the black power organizations. These leaflets often misrepresented the philosophy of the groups. The FBI hoped this would discourage people from joining or thinking favorably of the organizations. Periodically, false information on these groups was knowingly released to the news media.

Organization leaders were arrested repeatedly for minor, and sometimes made-up, charges. The arrests were meant to drain the organization's personal and financial resources and hinder its ability to act.

One COINTELPRO tactic had the odd-sounding code name "bad jacketing," and referred to a key individual becoming the subject of an FBI campaign to create suspicions about him or her within the organization. Once an individual was targeted for "bad jacketing," rumors were spread and evidence was made up. Sometimes there were attempts to convince other members that the targeted individual was an FBI informer.

COINTELPRO tactics were used against all of the black power groups active in the late 1960s and early 1970s. In all, there were 360 separate operations. But the most unrestrained use of these tactics was aimed at the Black Panther party.

THE BLACK PANTHERS

The Black Panthers originated in Oakland, California, in 1965. A large number of Oakland's black citizens believed that the police were racist. "Off the pigs," ("kill the police") became their unofficial slogan. They believed the police were purposely harassing them because they were black. They armed themselves and started following police cars to make sure they did nothing to harm blacks.

In 1967, one of the Panthers' most well-known leaders, Huey Newton, was wounded in a shoot-out that left one policeman dead. A poster of the Panther's Minister of Defense, holding a shotgun in one hand and a spear in the other, helped bring more national attention to the group.

The Black Panthers believed that "the white man's real power was its military force." They urged that a shotgun be kept in every black man's home.

Hoover felt that "the Black Panther party, without question, represents the greatest threat to the internal security of the country." He went on to say that they were "the most dangerous and violence-prone of all extremist groups."

Two Black Panther members outside of the California State Capitol

Hoover had the Black Panther party classified as a threat to the national security. This classification allowed the FBI to wiretap and use other electronic surveillance on the Black Panthers without court approval.

The director wanted to know what the Panthers were going to do before they did it. He wanted COINTELPRO tactics used to turn Panther leaders against one another. The FBI was successful in this attempt.

By 1969, the FBI was investigating all 42 chapters and 1,200 members of the Black Panther party for possible violations of the law. But the Panthers were now talking less about violence and more about helping the community in other ways. They were organizing tenant strikes, day-care centers, and health clinics. One of their most popular activities was the free breakfast for children program. The FBI made repeated attempts to disrupt and destroy these programs.

A Black Panther-run school

There were a number of shoot-outs between the police and the Panthers. The circumstances surrounding them caused some people to suspect that they were planned assassinations. One of these cases involved the FBI's COINTELPRO tactics as they were used against Fred Hampton and the Illinois chapter of the Black Panthers. The FBI's "Racial Matters Squad" had compiled 4,000 pages of information on Hampton, the nationally known chairman of the Illinois Black Panthers. The bureau had also placed an informer within Hampton's organization. He rose high enough to become Illinois Black Panther Party Chief of Security, as well as Hampton's bodyguard.

The informer did more than provide the FBI with information. He also encouraged the Panthers to commit criminal activity so that the police or the FBI might catch them in the act.

The informer gave the bureau a floor plan of Hampton's apartment. The FBI worked closely with the Chicago police in planning their December 4, 1969, raid.

At 4:30 A.M., fourteen Chicago policemen, supposedly looking for weapons, raided Hampton's apartment. They were armed with 27 guns, including 5 shotguns and a submachine gun. The police claimed they raided the house only after being fired on. But evidence shows that the Panthers fired only one shot, while the police fired between 83 and 99

Three members of the Black Panther party in front of the Chicago City Hall

shots. Forty-two were fired at Hampton's bed. He died in the raid.

There were many questions about the raid then, and the case remains a controversial one.

THE ANTIWAR MOVEMENT

Since 1954, the government of the United States had been increasing its military presence in Vietnam. During the administration of John F. Kennedy, most Americans had never heard of this small Southeast Asian country. That began to change in 1964. In August, Congress voted into law the "Tonkin Gulf Resolution." This gave President Lyndon Johnson the authority he needed to expand America's military activities in Vietnam. Only two congressmen voted against the resolution, accurately reflecting the nation's support for the president.

In November, 1964, LBJ was elected in a landslide victory over Senator Barry Goldwater. A significant factor in the election was the widely held belief that Johnson, unlike Goldwater, would not escalate the war.

But one year later, in 1965, Johnson launched "Operation Rolling Thunder," the sustained bombing of Communist North Vietnam. By the end of 1965, there were 180,000 Americans stationed in South Vietnam. This increased to 280,000 in 1966 and, by 1968, there were 500,000 Americans fighting in Vietnam.

More troops meant more casualties. The "body count" (the official military term for counting the dead) was mounting. In 1963, seventy-six Americans died in Vietnam. By the end of 1967, nearly 10,000 were killed and 100,000 wounded. Before the war was over (1975), 58,800 Americans would be killed and approximately 300,000 wounded. Each night, Americans watched the war on the nightly news programs. Shocked by the lengthening list of the dead — often loved ones and neighbors — and seeing no end to the suffering in sight, the American public began to turn against the war.

The first major demonstration against American military intervention in Vietnam was held on the Berkeley campus of the University of California in 1964. By 1965, there were rallies, speeches, protests, and "teach-ins" being staged at colleges across the country. Prominent Americans — writers, artists, musicians, scientists, physicians, religious leaders, professors, and politicians — joined the growing nucleus of antiwar demonstrators.

In November, 1965, Norman Morrison, a Quaker, burned himself to death in front of the Pentagon. Morrison, a father of three, did this in a desperate attempt to protest what he considered the killing of innocent Vietnamese children by the American military.

Protestors marched in the streets of London, Rome, Brussels, and other European cities. Twenty thousand turned out in San Francisco and one hundred twenty-five thousand marched in New York City to protest the war. In Washington, DC, government troops had to be called out to protect the Defense Department, which was surrounded by 50,000

Anti-Vietnam War demonstrations took place throughout the country.

protestors. Men burned their draft cards in public displays and saw themselves at night on the news.

By early January, 1968, there was a widening belief that the war was not going well. Despite assurances by the president, his cabinet members, and advisors, Americans in increasing numbers were expressing their dissatisfaction with the war.

In mid-March, Senator Eugene McCarthy polled a surprising 40 percent of the vote in the New Hampshire Democratic presidential primary. McCarthy had been an early outspoken critic of the president's policies in Vietnam. His strong showing in New Hampshire added fuel to the fire of the antiwar movement.

In Washington, DC, the president could hear the protestors on Pennsylvania Avenue chanting: "Hey, hey, LBJ, how many kids did you kill today?"

On the evening of March 31, 1968, President Lyndon Baines Johnson gave a televised speech. He stunned the nation when he closed by announcing that: "I shall not seek, and I will not accept, the nomination of my party for another term as your President."

Lyndon Johnson had been driven from office by the coming together of two forces: the heightened protest of black Americans coinciding, in the late 1960s, with a growing antiwar movement. As one analyst said, it was "as close to overthrowing the government as can happen within the American system."

THE FBI VS. WAR PROTESTERS

J. Edgar Hoover was outraged by the antiwar movement. Since the first peace demonstrations were held in 1965, Hoover employed the same tactics he had used against the communists fifteen years earlier. Thousands of informants were placed within the movement's various organizations. The antiwar groups depended on volunteers for a variety of

Antiwar protestors would sometimes chant: "Hey, hey, LBJ, how many kids did you kill today?"

jobs. Opposition to the war was the only requirement. Once these organizations were infiltrated, hidden microphones were put in place, phone lines tapped, mailing lists copied, and the names of financial contributors recorded.

Hoover supplied the president with information about scheduled demonstrations. At first, President Johnson had requested only that the FBI run name-checks on people who had written criticizing his Vietnam policy. (After a speech on Vietnam, Johnson asked Hoover to check on anyone who sent a negative telegram to the White House.) But soon the embattled president asked Hoover to do more.

Hoover advised Johnson, and stated publicly, that the communists were behind the antiwar movement. Hoover hoped this would discredit the demonstrators in the eyes of most Americans. But the charge was hard to believe. The protests appeared to be genuine and, at times, almost spontaneous. The participants seemed to represent an increasingly broad spectrum of the American population. Most, including members of the FBI hierarchy, were unconvinced by Hoover's arguments that the antiwar movement was communist controlled. William C. Sullivan, number three man in the FBI, believed that "There is only a tiny handful of antiwar people who have had contact with Communist nations. As far as American Communists are concerned, forget it. They are no longer important. Most of the young people who are against the war are simply that: young people who are patriotic but who are totally committed to seeing that the United States gets out of the war in Vietnam." (Sullivan was dismissed by Hoover in 1971.)

Switching gears, Hoover declared that this was a new kind of conspiracy "that is extremely subtle and devious and hence difficult to understand . . . a conspiracy reflected by questionable moods and attitudes, by unrestrained individualism, by nonconformism in dress and speech, even by obscene language, rather than by formal membership in existing organizations."

By 1968, the number of demonstrations had increased dramatically (from 400 to 34,000 within a year). The nature of the antiwar movement had changed as had the nature of the war. There was more civil disobedience (non-violently disobeying a law in order to effect change). In Oakland, California, protestors laid down in front of army trains carrying soldiers bound for Vietnam. Some antiwar groups had emerged with a more militant approach. They were, in fact, capable of violence. Even peaceful demonstrations were liable to erupt. Those who considered the antiwar protestors unpatriotic, and worse, began confronting them with hurled objects and clenched fists.

Hoover blamed the violence on the movement and its leaders. He considered them traitors in time of war. The antiwar demonstrations were convincing the communist North Vietnamese that the United States, due to pressure at home, would eventually withdraw from the war.

A demonstrator confronts National Guardsmen at an antiwar march against the Pentagon.

The movement against the Vietnam War began to draw Americans of all types.

Hoover had long been investigating groups that disagreed with President Johnson's Vietnam policy. But beginning in 1968, his efforts intensified and expanded in scope. Hoover went on the offensive. He actively sought to disrupt and destroy all opposition to the war. By 1968, Hoover had decided to initiate COINTELPRO tactics against the antiwar movement. Between 1968 and 1971, there were nearly three hundred separate COINTELPRO operations against antiwar organizations.

The FBI started to classify more and more antiwar groups as threats to the nation's security. The Security Index became the Rabble Rouser Index, the Agitator Index, and the Key Activist Index.

FBI informants printed, produced, and distributed leaflets that gave the wrong time and place for meetings and marches. When the FBI knew there was going to be a demonstration, they spread false rumors that there would be violence in hopes that this would discourage people from participating.

Phones were tapped and leaders were followed. If a well-known activist committed a federal crime, no matter how minor, he was charged with that crime. Agents were directed to increase the number of interviews with antiwar activists. Hoover wanted this done to "get the point across that there is an FBI agent behind every mailbox." He wanted to establish the same paranoia that he had in his attack on black organizations.

FBI agents using fake names called employers and told them of the antiwar activities of their employees in hopes they would be fired. "Mail covers" were routinely run. This involved intercepting letters at the post office, copying the address, the return address, and the postmark. But the bureau went further. They bribed building superintendents and obtained keys to mailboxes, took the mail, steamed open the envelopes, and read and photocopied the contents. Then they resealed the envelopes and returned the mail to the mailboxes.

Anonymous letters were written by the FBI to students' families and friends advising them of the radical activities of their loved ones — often mistakenly. Parents became frightened and worried: clearly the object of the FBI's tactics.

The homes of parents, family members, and friends of antiwar activists were broken into as the FBI searched for information. In cases of students who were fugitives, agents searched for information as to their whereabouts. Had their families gone to see them? The agents looked for airplane tickets, road maps, hotel names, anything that would tell them where the fugitives had fled to. In at least one case soil samples were taken from a bathtub in the hope that they could be analyzed and a location pinpointed.

But all of this wasn't enough for Hoover. He pushed his agents for more: "You are urged to take an enthusiastic and imaginative approach to this new counterintelligence endeavor and the bureau will be pleased to entertain any suggestions or techniques you might recommend."

President Johnson, Hoover's boss for the past few years, waived the director's mandatory retirement at 70 by issuing an executive order. Now, in 1968, Hoover was 73 and, to some, it seemed as if he would reign forever.

But to others, the end was in sight.

CHAPTER ELEVEN

★

THE CITIZENS' COMMISSION TO INVESTIGATE THE FBI

"One of the things that most people forget is that J. Edgar Hoover was just about as powerful as anyone in the United States of America. Congressmen were scared to death of him. They got brave after he died."

Former Attorney General Nicholas Katzenbach

"That man has been out of his mind for three years."

Former Attorney General Richard Kleindienst

In 1968, Republican Richard Nixon was elected the 37th President of the United States. Outgoing President Johnson had some advice for his successor: "Dick, you will come to depend on Edgar. He is a pillar of strength in a city of weak men. You will rely on him time and time again to maintain security. He's the only one you can put your complete trust in."

The newly elected president and the director had been political allies since the late 1940s when Nixon served on the House Committee on Un-American Activities. At that time, Hoover's cooperation allowed the freshman senator from California to gain national recognition as an anti-Communist. (In fact, Nixon and the FBI had a history that went back even further. In 1937, after graduating from Duke Law School, Richard Nixon applied for a job as an FBI agent. His application was denied because it was believed he lacked aggressiveness.)

181

President Richard Nixon and J. Edgar Hoover meeting in New York

Once Nixon became president, there was every expectation that the two men would work well together. But the events that would cause the downfall of both were being set in motion, although neither was aware of it.

It would begin for both with an illegal break-in. One took place in an exclusive Washington, DC, apartment complex, the Watergate. For Richard Nixon it was the first step on a road that would lead to his becoming the only president of the United States to resign from office.

Another burglary, that of a small FBI resident agency, would mark the beginning of the end for the director of the Federal Bureau of Investigation.

President Richard Nixon bids farewell to the White House following his resignation.

The following *New York Times* story out of Philadelphia appeared on March 10, 1971:

F.B.I. REPORTS OFFICE RAID

> The Federal Bureau of Investigation office at Media near here was raided early today and Government property removed, according to an F.B.I. spokesman. In an anonymous telephone call to a Philadelphia reporter, a group calling itself the Citizens' Commission to Investigate the F.B.I. said it had "removed all the records."

When FBI agents reported for work on the morning of March 9, 1971, they discovered hundreds of files missing. Although there were secure filing cabinets available, they were filled with the agents' equipment such as guns, handcuffs, and ID cards, rather than important files. The documents the burglars were looking for were in an unlocked safe. Only two agents were assigned to the Media, Pennsylvania, office. They used a one-room office on the second floor of a county building. There was no alarm system.

A small, disciplined, secret group — the Citizens' Commission to Investigate the FBI — had taken the documents. The Citizens' Commission is believed to have been an antiwar group of no more than twenty people. They were very careful about how they conducted their business. The group carefully selected and released certain stolen documents to chosen congressmen and newspapers in the coming weeks. These documents had been photocopied in batches at different locations. The copies were sent from mailboxes around the country. (Friends of group members, unaware of the contents, were asked to mail envelopes while on trips.)

Soon excerpts began appearing in *The Washington Post* and *The New York Times*. By the end of the month, an 82-page excerpt of the documents appeared in an antiwar journal. It was the first time FBI files were read by the general public. They showed the extremes of Hoover's COINTELPRO activities.

Many of the 800 files related to FBI investigations, surveillances, and harassment of college students suspected of antiwar activities. The breadth and type of tactics used by the FBI against young American citizens who were not accused of any crime was a shocking revelation to many. The documents showed that the FBI devoted a good portion of its resources to doing battle with Americans whose politics were considered a threat by J. Edgar Hoover to the national security. What was once the claim of a relatively small group of critics, was now known by all citizens.

Hoover reacted furiously. Roy Moore was placed in charge of the investigation code-named MEBURG (for Media Burglary). He was joined by other top investigators who worked on the case for months. It was one of the most intensive investigations in FBI history. (To date, no member of the Citizens' Commission to Investigate the FBI has been apprehended, and the case has never been solved.)

Hoover threatened to close all 538 resident agencies, and, in fact, did close over 100. He feared that they might be broken into with similar ease. He ordered that greater security precautions be taken in FBI offices throughout the country. Hundreds of thousands of dollars were spent on these improvements. All COINTELPRO activities were suspended immediately.

But it was too late. The truth was out and, to many, both in and out of government, it was shocking.

In April, 1971, Majority Leader Hale Boggs, a longtime Hoover ally, verbally attacked the director on the floor of the House of Representatives:

> The time has come for the Attorney General of the United States to ask for the resignation of Mr. Hoover. . . . When the FBI taps the telephones of Members of this body and of Members of the Senate, when the FBI stations agents on college campuses to infiltrate college organizations, when the FBI adopts the tactics of the Soviet Union and Hitler's Gestapo, then it is time . . . that the present Director no longer be the Director.

Days after this speech, *Life* ran a cover story entitled: "The 47-Year Reign of J. Edgar Hoover: Emperor of the FBI." Weeks after that, *Newsweek*'s cover story said it was "Time for a Change."

There was public pressure on the bureau to make a full disclosure of its illegal activities. The House and Senate formed a committee to investigate the bureau. Polls showed that one out of every two Americans believed Hoover should retire. His prestige had fallen to an all-time low.

On May 2, 1972, a year after the Media, Pennsylvania, burglary, J. Edgar Hoover died of a heart attack. He was 77.

President Richard Nixon ordered a state funeral with military honors.

The director of the FBI at one of his last public appearances

BIBLIOGRAPHY

Alexander, Shana. *The Pizza Connection*. NY: Weidenfeld and Nicholson, 1988.

Blumenthal, Ralph. *Last Days of the Sicilians*. NY: Times Books, 1988.

Branch, Taylor. *Parting the Waters*. NY: Simon & Schuster, 1989.

Buitrago, Anne Mari and Leon Andrew Immerman. *Are You Now or Have You Ever Been in the FBI Files?* NY: Grove Press, 1981.

Burns, James MacGregor. *The Crosswinds of Freedom*. NY: Alfred A. Knopf, 1989.

Cagin, Seth and Phillip Dray. *We Are Not Afraid*. NY: Macmillan, 1988.

Caute, David. *The Great Fear*. NY: Simon & Schuster, 1978.

Churchill, Ward and Jim Vander Wall. *Agents of Repression*. Boston: South End Press, 1988.

Cook, Fred J. *The FBI Nobody Knows*. NY: Macmillan, 1964.

Cooper, Courtney Riley. *Ten Thousand Public Enemies*. Boston: Little, Brown, 1935.

Demaris, Ovid. *The Director: An Oral Biography of J. Edgar Hoover*. NY: Harper's Magazine Press, 1975.

Drasnin, Irv. *The American Experience:* A film documentary written and produced by Drasnin Production, Inc. for THE AMERICAN EXPERIENCE, WGBH Educational Foundation, and WNET/Thirteen, 1991.

Garrow, David J. *The FBI and Martin Luther King*. NY: W. W. Norton, 1981.

———. *Bearing the Cross*. NY: Random House, 1986.

Gentry, Curt. *J. Edgar Hoover: The Man and the Secrets*. NY: W. W. Norton, 1991.

Goodman, Walter. *The Committee*. NY: Farrar, Straus & Giroux, 1968.

Hoover, J. Edgar. *Masters of Deceit*. NY: Henry Holt, 1958.

———. *A Study of Communism*. NY: Holt, Rinehart and Winston, 1962.

Huie, William Bradford. *Three Lives for Mississippi*. London: Heinemann, 1965.

Kennedy, Ludovic. *The Airman and the Carpenter*. NY: Viking, 1985.

Look, editors. *The Official History of the FBI*. NY: Dutton, 1947.

Look, editors. *The Story of the FBI*. NY: Dutton, 1947.

Lowenthal, Max. *The Federal Bureau of Investigation*. NY: Sloan, 1950.

Mason, Alpheus Thomas. *Harlan Fiske Stone*. NY: Viking, 1956.

Navasky, Victor. *Kennedy Justice*. NY: Atheneum, 1971.

Nixon, Richard M. *Six Crises*. Garden City: Doubleday, 1962.

O'Reilly, Kenneth. *Racial Matters: The FBI's Secret File on Black America 1960–1972*. NY: The Free Press, 1989.

Overstreet, Harry and Bonaro. *The FBI in Our Open Society*. NY: W. W. Norton, 1969.

Pistone, Joseph D. with Richard Woodley. *Donnie Brasco: My Undercover Life in the Mafia*. NY: New American Library, 1987.

Powers, Richard Gid. *Secrecy and Power: The Life of J. Edgar Hoover*. NY: The Free Press, 1987.

Quimby, Myron. *The Devil's Emissaries*. NJ: Barnes, 1969.

Stone, I.F. *In Time of Torment 1961–1967*. Boston: Little, Brown, 1967.

———. *The Haunted Fifties 1953–1963*. Boston: Little, Brown, 1963.

Sullivan, William C. *The Bureau: My 30 Years in Hoover's FBI*. NY: W. W. Norton, 1979.

Theoharis, Athan and John Stuart Cox. *The Boss: J. Edgar Hoover and the Great American Inquisition*. Philadelphia: Temple University Press, 1988.

Turner, William W. *Hoover's FBI*. LA: Sherbourne Press, 1970.

Unger, Sanford. *FBI*. Boston: Little, Brown, 1975.

Wade, Wyn Craig. *The Fiery Cross—The Ku Klux Klan in America*. NY: Simon & Schuster, 1987.

Waller, George. *Kidnap: The Story of the Lindbergh Case*. NY: Dial Press, 1961.

Watters, Pat and Stephen Gillars. *Investigating the FBI*. Garden City: Doubleday, 1963.

Weinstein, Allen. *Perjury: The Hiss–Chambers Case*. NY: Alfred A. Knopf, 1978.

Whitehead, Don. *The FBI Story*. NY: Random House, 1956.

Wicker, Tom. "What Have They Done Since They Shot Dillinger?" *New York Times Magazine*, December 28, 1969.

TIMELINE

1895 J. Edgar Hoover is born.

1901 Theodore Roosevelt becomes president.

1908 Bureau of Investigation is founded.

1909 William Taft becomes president.

1913 Woodrow Wilson becomes president.

Hoover graduates from high school.

1917 United States enters World War I.

Hoover receives his law degree. He takes his first job in the Justice Department.

The Russian Revolution establishes a communist government.

1918 World War I ends.

1919 The Eighteenth Amendment (Prohibition) is ratified.

Hoover is appointed head of the General Intelligence Division.

1920 The "Palmer Raids" are launched.

1921 Warren G. Harding becomes president.

Hoover is named assistant director of the Bureau of Investigation.

1923 Calvin Coolidge becomes president.

1924 Hoover is appointed director of the Bureau of Investigation.

1929 Seven men are killed in the St. Valentine's Day Massacre.

Herbert Hoover becomes president.

The stock market crashes.

1932 Lindbergh baby is kidnapped.

1933 Franklin D. Roosevelt becomes president.

Eighteenth Amendment is repealed.

1934 John Dillinger is killed by bureau agents.

1935 The name of the bureau is changed to the Federal Bureau of Investigation.

The FBI's National Academy holds its first session.

1939 Germany invades Poland and World War II begins.

1941 Japanese attack Pearl Harbor and the United States enters the war.

1945 Harry S. Truman becomes president.

Germany surrenders.

U.S. drops atomic bombs on the Japanese cities of Hiroshima and Nagasaki. The Japanese surrender.

1948 Whittaker Chambers appears before the House Committee on Un-American Activities.

1950 Senator Joseph McCarthy delivers a speech claiming that there are communists in the State Department.

The Korean War begins.

1953 Julius and Ethel Rosenberg are electrocuted for spying.

The Korean War ends.

1954 The Supreme Court rules that segregation in public schools is unconstitutional.

1955 In Montgomery, Alabama, a bus boycott, led by Martin Luther King, Jr., begins.

1957 Martin Luther King, Jr., with others, forms the Southern Christian Leadership Conference.

1958 *Masters of Deceit*, by J. Edgar Hoover, becomes a bestseller.

1961 John F. Kennedy becomes president.

1963 John F. Kennedy is assassinated; Lyndon Baines Johnson becomes president.

1964 Congress passes the Tonkin Gulf Resolution giving President Johnson the power to wage war in Vietnam.

Martin Luther King, Jr., receives the Nobel Peace Prize.

FBI agents arrest members of the Ku Klux Klan for their involvement in the murders of three civil rights workers in Mississippi.

1965   *The FBI* begins a nine-year, prime-time run on ABC TV.

1968   President Johnson announces he will not run for reelection.

Martin Luther King, Jr., is assassinated.

Robert Kennedy is assassinated.

1969   Richard Nixon becomes president.

1971   The Citizens' Commission to Investigate the FBI breaks into bureau offices in Media, Pennsylvania.

1972   J. Edgar Hoover dies at the age of 77.

The Watergate break-in takes place.

INDEX

Page references in italics indicate material in illustrations or photographs.

PHOTO CREDITS